DEVELOPING A HEALTHY
PRAYER LIFE

D1111895

DEVELOPING A HEALTHY
PRAYER LIFE

31 Meditations on Communing with God

James W. Beeke
and
Joel R. Beeke

Reformation Heritage Books
Grand Rapids, Michigan

Developing a Healthy Prayer Life
©2010 by James W. Beeke and Joel R. Beeke

Published by
REFORMATION HERITAGE BOOKS
2965 Leonard St., NE
Grand Rapids, MI 49525
616-977-0889 / Fax 616-285-3246
e-mail: orders@heritagebooks.org
website: www.heritagebooks.org

Printed in the United States of America
14 15 16 17 18 19/10 9 8 7 6 5 4

Library of Congress Cataloging-in-Publication Data

Beeke, James W.
  Developing a healthy prayer life : 31 meditations on commun-
ing with God / James W. Beeke and Joel R. Beeke.
      p. cm.
  ISBN 978-1-60178-112-3 (pbk. : alk. paper) 1. Prayer—
Christianity. I. Beeke, Joel R., 1952- II. Title.
  BV210.3.B44 2010
  248.3'2—dc22
                                    2010043085

*For additional Reformed literature, request a free book list
from Reformation Heritage Books at the above address.*

CONTENTS

FOREWORD

I wish this book had fallen into my hands fifty years ago when I was a young Christian, but now I have it and have profited from it, realizing that its lessons, basic, true, and energizing, are relevant for disciples of the Lord Jesus at every age. I am thinking this moment of a housewife to whom I spoke earlier this week. She has just begun to attend the congregation and has the simplest faith. She is beginning to read Christian books; she is strong in her moral convictions, but her understanding of the faith is only beginning to be shaped. I promised that I would give five Christian books to her to help her first steps in this new pilgrimage. This book will certainly be one of them.

Alexander Whyte once said that if you wanted to humble a Christian you asked him about his praying. Ah, yes. One chats on about praying, its challenge and our struggles, but even today, as our journey draws to a close, we feel like a man picking up a pebble on the shores of a vast ocean. How little we know of communion with Father, Son, and Holy Spirit! We can define what prayer is. We can make our confession in the words of that immense statement, "It is impotence reaching out to omnipotence." Yet we are not left to stumble on blindly and find our own way. There is much instruction in the Bible's plain teaching on the nature of praying, warnings about hypocritical praying, and the examples of the psalmists, the apostles, and our Lord Himself. After the way of salvation, the theme most common in Scripture is the nature of true praying. Why is all this full detail given us if we did not need to be educated, strengthened, and stimulated to pray and not grow weary?

The cry from so many congregations is that the pulpit should be simpler. True, but not at the cost of simplistic repetition, wearying the people of God, telling the congregation what they have long known with no fresh stimulation. That is bad instruction. Should there not be one fresh thought in each sermon? Is that too much to ask? That is where this book is deceptive. Its stated aim is the instruction and encouragement of new Christians in their praying, and in this it succeeds admirably. The authors say, in effect, "We write to you, dear children, because you have known the Father" (1 John 2:13). But in speaking to them, their parents in the faith, old, mature Christians, overhear as it were, read, and are much helped as I have been.

I thank God for this book, and am glad that it will be the beginning of a new series of books, each of which contains thirty-one short meditations on a given subject—sufficient for a month's worth of daily devotionals. I hope that future books in this series will maintain the same standard of warmth, freshness, and lucidity, eminently suited to take the new-born generation of believers through the twenty-first century. I pray that this and future books will be greatly used, and become a classic series for new believers.

I pray that God will use *Developing a Healthy Prayer Life* exceedingly abundantly above what I am thinking now. The authors have vast experience in Christian nurture and communication. I have nothing but hope that since they have been given by Heaven (I believe) a conviction of the need for such plain, affectionate books and the grace to write them, that God the Holy Spirit will take and use them for the good of His people this whole world over.

—GEOFF THOMAS

WHAT IS PRAYER?

You are about to embark on a journey through a most important part of Christian life and experience, the development of a healthy prayer life. So what is prayer?

Prayer is the act of forging a connection between two specific points: our human needs and the resources of God offered to us in Christ. You can start at either point, and reach to the other in prayer.

True Christians have discovered that God, in Christ, offers them grace, mercy, pardon, peace, life, and love. This is revealed in the gospel, or "good news" of Jesus Christ (2 Peter 1:2–4). And true Christians have experienced how much they need these things—indeed, how the heart cries out for them in prayer (Ps. 84:2).

Prayer identifies the desires of the heart and expresses them to God. It can be silent or spoken. It can be as simple as "God be merciful to me a sinner" (Luke 18:13) or as detailed as the high-priestly prayer of Christ (John 17), in which He poured out everything He wanted God the Father to give to those who believe in the Lord Jesus Christ. It can even take the form of a song. The Psalms are called "the prayers of David" (Ps. 72:20).

Christian prayer embraces God's will as revealed in Scripture for its rule or guide. The goal is to ask for things in harmony with what God wants for us. God's covenant promises, sealed with the blood of Christ (1 Cor. 11:25), are the surest foundation for prayer (2 Cor. 1:20). When divine and human wills agree according to God's rule, prayer will surely be answered (1 John 5:14–15).

Christian prayer develops as believers come to trust in Christ more and more for all they need or are called to do, even to know how to pray or to ask for grace to keep on praying. We have no claim on God but must rely entirely on the merit and prayers of Christ and the indispensable aid of the Holy Spirit (Rom. 8:26). That is why Christ commands us to "ask in my name" (John 15:16; 16:24).

Christian prayer is also part of our repentance from sin. In prayer, we confess our sins, asking God to forgive those sins and to provide the strength we need to forsake them and kill them. From God's perspective, a sin truly confessed is a sin forgiven (Ps. 32:5). What's more, the same God who forgives sin cleanses from all unrighteousness (1 John 1:9).

Finally, Christian prayer is an act of worship (Ps. 65:1–2). As we come to know God in Christ, we are moved to praise Him as Almighty God and our Father in heaven. As we experience God's work in our daily lives, we learn to thank Him for the many good and perfect gifts He offers us as mercies from His fatherly hand (James 1:17). We also learn to rejoice in trials, hardships, loss, and sorrow, since these come to us not by chance but according to God's will to accomplish His purpose for us (Rom. 8:28, 29).

We have much to learn to have a truly healthy prayer life. Pray for grace to open your heart to the Word and Spirit of God to receive the counsel of these meditations with a teachable mind and a moldable conscience. Begin now by praying for an understanding heart and grace to grow in the knowledge of Christ.

WHO SHOULD PRAY?

Seek ye the LORD while he may be found, call ye upon him while he is near: let the wicked forsake his way, and the unrighteous man his thoughts: and let him return unto the LORD, and he will have mercy upon him; and to our God, for he will abundantly pardon.
— ISAIAH 55:6 –7

In Isaiah 55, God shows His compassion by inviting "everyone that thirsteth" (v. 1) to enter into His promised blessings. This thirst of deep spiritual longing drives us to Him for mercy; verses 6 and 7 emphasize the urgency of responding to Him. The verb *seek* suggests actively using God's means of prayer. The One we seek is the LORD: the unchangeable, gracious, covenant-keeping Jehovah. We should not foolishly delay embracing God's offer; we must seek Him "while he may be found"—*now*—before the day of our death. The prophet emphasizes personal prayer with the words "call ye," reminding us that God's offered salvation is available now, while "He is near" us with His Word and blessings. We must not reject this offer. If we do not heed the call, the time will come when He will not be found and we will be separated from Him forever. God requires us wholeheartedly to repent of our sinful thoughts, words, and actions, receiving by faith His abundant, pardoning mercy and grace, which far exceed the mountains of our great sin and guilt.

Some people argue that because they cannot pray rightly, it is better for them not to pray at all. They draw support from Scripture verses that describe the prayers and worship of sinners as a stench in God's nostrils and an abomination in His sight. They say that God will not hear sinners and that whatever is not of faith is sin.

The first part of this argument—that we cannot pray rightly—is true, but the conclusion that it is then better not to pray at all is false. If such reasoning were valid, then we could draw similar conclusions about all sorts of spiritual activities. Can I read the Bible in the right way? If not, I had better not read it. Can I sing psalms and hymns in the right way? If not, I had better not sing them. Can I attend church in the right way? If not, I had better not go. This reasoning, if it were true, would actually keep believers from praying more than unbelievers, since believers feel their sinful infirmities more. Are the converted or the unconverted more acquainted with their unworthiness? Who truly recognizes what an abomination and offense he is to God? Who fully acknowledges that he is a sinner who lacks faith? Who understands that God has every right not to hear his prayer—the converted or unconverted? This type of argument, which sounds pious, is really an irreligious excuse and a perversion of the gospel message. It is dangerous to believe, teach, or imply that we may not pray until we are whole or that we may approach God only when we are spiritually upright. Psalm 130:3–4 encourages the guilty who cannot stand before God to come to Him: "If thou, LORD, shouldest mark iniquities, O Lord, who shall stand? But there is forgiveness with thee, that thou mayest be feared."

The gospel calls poor, lame, and blind sinners, those who are full of sin and putrefying spiritual sores, to come to Christ for healing—to Him who delights in showing mercy and love to miserable creatures. Luther once said, "Being saved is getting lost at Jesus' feet." Satan's ultimate goal is to keep sinners from Jesus Christ. If he cannot accomplish this as a roaring lion, he will attempt to do so as an angel of light. If you are deeply concerned to know whether the genuine work of the Holy Spirit or the deceptive work of Satan is in your heart, test it by this scriptural key: the former draws you toward Christ while the latter strives to keep you from Christ.

We sin when we sing psalms, attend church, read Scripture, or pray and our heart is not right with God. But we sin doubly when our heart is not only sinful but we also neglect using God's gift of prayer. We cannot deny man's sinfulness, as revealed by God's law; we are sinful, polluted, and an abomination in God's sight. But we also must not deny God's gospel; He delights to save sinners and encourages them to come to Him (John 6:37). Both these truths should not keep us from Jesus Christ, but direct us to Him, the only remedy for sin. The gospel should lead us to pray, "God, be merciful to me, a sinner. Please take away all the unrighteousness of self that fills me and fill me with all that I am missing—the righteousness of Jesus Christ."

God spoke to the *entire* house of Israel, "I will yet for this be enquired of" (Ezek. 36:37). "Seek *ye* the LORD." You are too sinful not to pray; sinners are the very people who need prayer. Therefore, pray.

2

PRAY IN CHRIST'S NAME

Hitherto have ye asked nothing in my name: ask, and ye shall receive, that your joy may be full.

—JOHN 16:24

Though we frequently end our prayers with "for Jesus' sake," we often pray for our own sake. Although we condemn the doctrine of salvation by our own good works and believe in salvation by grace based upon Christ's merits, this truth is often missing in a practical way in our daily prayer life.

We tend to think that when we have warm feelings, a lively sense of deep reverence, a feeling of heart humility, a close sense of God's presence, or real earnestness for the Lord, that God will then hear our prayer. If we reason this way, on what foundation are we basing our judgment? Do we truly believe that God will hear our prayer for Jesus' sake, or for ours? Do we think that God will be pleased, on the basis of our feelings, to give us what we have asked for? Do we believe that our prayers themselves deserve to be heard, answered, and rewarded by a perfect God, who can only be pleased by perfect righteousness? If so, we are denigrating the perfections of God—His divine attributes—to our own level and thereby insulting His holy, infinite Being.

Praying in the name of Christ is to not base my hope and expectation of being heard upon the merits of my "good" prayers. Rather, it is to pray putting all my trust in Jesus Christ's merits and His intercession. Sometimes we feel that our prayers are so poor and lacking so much that we despair of an audience with the Lord. There can be so little persevering, thanking, and felt need in our prayers that we conclude that God will never hear them. Reasoning like this displays a lack of praying "for Jesus' sake." It testifies of unbelief in God's grace and love for undeserving sinners.

Jesus taught us, "Hitherto have ye asked nothing in my name" (John 16:24). To pray in Christ's name is to take refuge in Him as God's beloved Son—the One whom the Father delights to hear and to honor. Praying in Jesus' name includes confessing who is truly God and Master in my life. While we condemn praying to idols as being foolish, how many times do we not pray to the idol of self? We often bow our knees to our god of self. Satan tempted Jesus by saying, "Bow down and worship me." Think of what a degrading insult this was to God! Our prayers can testify that we are looking to the god of self with the attitude that we are lord and master. We even dare to tell God to do our bidding. We act as though we are Lord and God is our servant. Have you ever felt guilty of this in your prayers and been arrested in prayer of your self-centered idolatry?

One of the reasons why we can ask and not receive is because we ask in our own name. This would be similar to a child who asks his parent for something, but his asking is not based on need or the parent's judgment and willingness to give. Instead, his asking is based selfishly upon one or two things he did to help around the house. Because of this, he now thinks he has the right to tell his parents exactly what he wants them to do, even how and when they should do it. If his parents truly love this child, will they respond to his selfish demands in the way and at the time that he wants it?

One clear evidence of this problem in Christians' prayer lives is when we spend more time preparing to come to Christ than in actually coming to Him. Parents, what would you think of your child who had a need, but spent hours getting himself ready, thinking of how to say things in a perfect way, working up all the right feelings, showing all the right mannerisms, and then hoping, maybe, that you will be willing to hear him? Would this honor or insult you and your love for your child?

Praying in Christ's name requires repudiating praying in our own name. It not only testifies of our status as sinners but also of Christ's status as Savior—of our sin, and His grace! No wonder Scripture lovingly commands us to pray in the name of Christ.

PRAY BELIEVINGLY

And Jesus answering saith unto them, Have faith in God. For verily I say unto you, That whosoever shall say unto this mountain, Be thou removed, and be thou cast into the sea; and shall not doubt in his heart, but shall believe that those things which he saith shall come to pass; he shall have whatsoever he saith. Therefore I say unto you, What things soever ye desire, when ye pray, believe that ye receive them, and ye shall have them.

—MARK 11:22–24

Faith speaks of believing and trusting. Trusting is acting upon belief. For example, we can *believe* that a plank over a stream will hold our weight. Actually walking over the plank reveals our *trust*. True faith is trusting my life with all its cares in God's hands. Do I believe that the Lord knows what is best for me, or that I know best? Do I become upset and distrust God when I fear that He will not do things my way, or am I upset and distrust myself when I do not do things God's way?

Prayer requires faith: *believing* in God, *trusting* in God, and *placing our expectations* in God. When trusting in God, we must believe "that he is" (Heb. 11:6) as well as who He says He is. We must believe His Word. When we trust God, we desire His will to conquer our will so that it aligns with His. When we place our expectations in God, we attest and believe that God is almighty, and our hearts strive to be one with God's will.

Verse 22 emphasizes that we must have faith *first*. We need to desire God and His will, in order to pray according to it. When we do not pray in faith, we pray for the wrong mountains to be removed. Many mountains exist—not only mountains of outward problems, but also mountains of our own sinful, personal desires, plans, and thoughts. These mountains often oppose God's plan and the promotion of His kingdom. James writes, "Ye ask, and receive not, because ye ask amiss," not according to God's will, but "that ye may consume it upon your lusts," placing your own will in the foreground (James 4:3).

When we pray believingly, we not only place our faith in God, but also in His will as expressed in His Word (John 17:17) and His promises (1 John 5:14–15). Do you believe that God is true to His Word and promises, that He will bless His Word and promises so that they will bring forth fruit?

Do you exercise faith in Christ when you pray (John 14:1)? Do you trust in His person and mediatorial work, looking for Him to meet all your needs as your Prophet, Priest, and King? Do you rest in His natures, states, and benefits as inseparable from your salvation? Are you concerned for the cause of Christ's kingdom, the promotion of His Name and His truth, that these may shape your own desires and purposes, and consume your time and energy? God's will becomes primary and your will becomes secondary when true faith is active in your life. A living faith will generate heartfelt desires to be conformed to His will.

Do you actively place your faith in Christ? A business-man who sends out trade ships believes they will return with rich merchandise. Are you looking for fruits today? Do you have godly expectations for this week? It is easy to focus on the mountains surrounding us: mountains of unbelief, worldly enticements, wrong doctrinal teachings and balance, and our own poor understandings and limited abilities. But we are also called to focus upon who God is in Christ—One who is greater than all these mountains. We are called to pray believingly, for Christ's sake. This is possible only when we are praying according to God's will, praying that His kingdom may come. Then we may believe, yes, are called to believe, that the mountains that stand in the way will be cast into the sea of oblivion.

Is not God faithful and trustworthy? Has He not faithfully cared for our families and churches? Has He not provided us with abundant testimony in His providence as well as in His Word? Do you truly believe in free and sovereign grace? Can the mighty mountains of your sin, unbelief, and hardened hearts withstand the almighty grace of God? Do you believe that God can cast your mountains of sin into the sea of His forgiveness by His free and sovereign grace? We are called to pray believingly.

PRAY PRIVATELY

But thou, when thou prayest, enter into thy closet, and when thou hast shut thy door, pray to thy Father which is in secret; and thy Father which seeth in secret shall reward thee openly.

—MATTHEW 6:6

Matthew 6:6 does not ask whether or not we should pray. Jesus clearly states, "*When* thou prayest." He uses the words "thou," "thy," and "thee" eight times in this one verse, emphasizing that prayer is to be a personal matter for each of us. Jesus places a double emphasis on the importance of privacy in personal prayer. He not only instructs His listeners to enter their closet (private quarters) to pray, but He also tells them to pray behind the closed door of that closet. Jesus underscores our need to be alone with God.

This marks an important distinction between upright and hypocritical religion. The hypocrite looks more to man than to God, but the upright person cares more for God than for man. We never read that Pharaoh, Saul, Judas, or Demas were seriously occupied with private prayer. A Pharisee desires to pray where people can see and hear him praying. He therefore prays on street corners or while standing in front of the temple. He is more interested in establishing a good name before men than a good conscience before God.

There are five main benefits attached to private prayer. The first is that private prayer is our prime opportunity to confess private sins. It is safe and wise to tell God things that would be unfit to tell others. Private prayer is communion with God, an unburdening of our souls to the One who already knows the secrets of our hearts.

Second, a sign of true love and friendship is when two people treasure time to be alone to talk together. So it is with the Lord and true believers. They love to hear each other's voice. This involves a double grace — not only that a sinner loves to hear Christ's voice, but also that Christ loves to hear a sinner's voice. Solomon wrote, "Let me see thy countenance, let me hear thy voice; for sweet is thy voice" (Song 2:14). Here the poet speaks of intimate friendship, especially of intimate communion in private prayer between Christ and the Christian.

Third, as friends love to share treasured secrets, so the Lord loves to share secrets of His truth, His Triune Person, His kingdom, and His love with believers. Through His Spirit He uncovers scriptural truth more deeply in the soul by means of private prayer. It is between the closest friends that the most is shared: "The secret of the LORD is with them that fear him; and he will shew them his covenant" (Ps. 25:14).

A fourth benefit attached to private prayer is that of knowing God more deeply. God reveals Himself most often to those who commune with Him in secret and will reward them openly in this life and in the life to come. Think of the things that were revealed to Daniel, Cornelius, Peter, and John as they were engaged in private prayer. Think of the power of private prayer—of the mercies granted and the judgments removed! Private prayer is the key to the treasure house of God's character, mercies, and purposes.

Private prayer, lastly, is also the path to a proven shelter, a haven of rest, a mighty fortress, a rock of defense for present adversities and an unknown future. Prayer is a refuge from the storms of life. This is why Satan fears and hates private prayer and will fight with every possible device and argument to keep you from prayer. The lives of Bible saints amply testify of this truth.

He who does not pray privately is his own thief and murderer. He robs himself of the greatest of blessings and kills his own spiritual life. Every newborn child cries for its mother; every spiritually newborn child of God calls out to Him. Can it be said of you as was said of Saul at Damascus, "Behold, he prayeth" (Acts 9:11b)?

PRAY SUBMISSIVELY

Then saith he unto them, My soul is exceeding sorrowful, even unto death: tarry ye here, and watch with me. And he went a little farther, and fell on his face, and prayed, saying, O my Father, if it be possible, let this cup pass from me: nevertheless not as I will, but as thou wilt.... He went away again the second time, and prayed, saying, O my Father, if this cup may not pass away from me, except I drink it, thy will be done.

— MATTHEW 26:38–39, 42

This portion of Scripture reveals a perfect example of true submission in prayer. When you pray, is your prayer more "Lord, do *my* will," or "Lord, help me submit to *Thy* will"? Do your prayers convey a view of yourself as master and God as servant: "Lord, do this according to my desires"? Are your prayers centered more on your being served, or on you serving? Do you pray that you might become a more faithful servant, unconditionally performing the will of your Master?

Suppose someone you love is seriously ill. Should you ask the Lord to restore this person to health? Yes, you may bring all your needs to the Lord. But do you also experience a deeper need? Do you pray in this way: "Lord, grant me the grace I need to serve, honor, and trust Thee—to rest in Thy will. Please grant that my dear one may recover, that I might rejoice in Thy deeds; but if not, grant that I may worship Thee. Above all, O Lord, I desire that Thy will be done."

In submissive prayer, we acknowledge that God knows more than we do. He has deeper reasons, purposes, and leadings in view than we can presently see or imagine. So often we act as director. We imagine that we know the right time, the best way, and exactly how our prayer should be answered. We may even tell God what He should do, struggling to convince and direct the Lord to do things according to our plans. In so doing, we lose the wonderful peace of submission.

When a young child runs to his father to talk about all his troubles and needs, does the child tell his father how to handle the situation and solve his problems? Does the child order his father to first do this and then that? Of course not. We experience true, childlike comfort when we rest in faith that our heavenly Father knows best. All we need to do is tell Him our needs. He knows what is best to do. This is the spirit of true submission that is revealed in childlike faith.

To do God's will, to glorify His Name, should be our deepest desire in prayer. The heartbeat of true prayer is to glorify God. True prayer pleads for following grace—grace to follow the Lord even when He leads in paths of adversity, sickness, or death. Submissive prayer desires to do God's will more than our own.

People frequently and mistakenly portray faith and submission as opposites: faith, they say, is confidence that God will answer a specific prayer in a specific way, while submission quietly accepts anything that comes. Someone might ask, "Doesn't faith expect God to answer prayer?" Yes, it does, but faith expects and desires God's answer, not my answer. Submission humbly receives what the omniscient Lord grants.

The Lord Jesus beautifully and perfectly lived out true, submissive prayer. When He faced the greatest of trials that any person ever faced, so that His sweat broke forth as blood and His soul was "exceeding sorrowful even unto death," falling on His face in anguish on the ground, He prayed. In childlike submission, He addressed God, "O my Father." When He said, "if it be possible," He did not ask what He desired, but what was possible according to the Father's will. Even though He knew perfectly the bitter cup He would drink—"let this cup pass from me"—He could neverthe-less say "not as I will, but as thou wilt" (Matt. 26:39). His deepest desire was to do the Father's will.

We must never let our thoughts or desires override God's will for our lives. What a blessing it is to follow in the foot-steps of the Master! May His example be reflected in our prayers and our lives. Pray for grace to pray submissively, "Thy will be done."

PRAY HUMBLY

God be merciful to me, a sinner.
—LUKE 18:13

The publican begins his prayer by addressing God. He was sincerely impressed with who God is as a holy and righteous Being. He scarcely dared to enter, to come into God's presence in His sanctuary. He did not even raise his eyes. Rather, he stood at the very back of the temple; he understood that it was a wonder he could be there at all.

It is one thing to say, "I am the least," or "I am satisfied with the lowest place," but it is something else to live this truth. The difference is evident in the fruit. The "talker" is proud of his humility, despises others, and feels superior—spiritually superior. But the "doer" internalizes this great wonder: "If I may be in the temple, if mercy is possible for *me*, then it is possible for anyone." God and His grace come first in the life and prayers of the humble believer.

The publican asks, "God be merciful to me." His petition for mercy portrays humility. True humility is produced by understanding who God is and who I am. In humble prayer the sinner relies on God's mercy as his only hope. The word "mercy" means showing love to someone who does not deserve it, loving someone, even an enemy, who has brought himself into a miserable condition and has no right to expect mercy. Mercy is an act of compassion.

When you sigh, "If only my prayer were a true prayer," you must be cautioned, because this thought can contain the notion that the *quality* of your prayer gives it merit. Humble petitioners know that their prayers have no merit. If you believed that your prayers were "good" prayers, then they would be prayers of self-merit. You would then be trusting in your prayer offerings, instead of God's gracious reception—trusting in your works instead of God's mercy. If you are waiting to approach God until you can offer "good" or "true" prayers, you are waiting in vain. Humility evaporates when it recognizes itself. The humble person is one who recognizes his pride. A humble person does not see his own prayer as humble. Praying humbly is asking, "God *be merciful*."

The publican's words "to me" emphasize prayer as a personal matter between God and my soul. The original Greek expresses the words "*a* sinner" more emphatically as "*the* sinner." I am not only a sinner, in the sense of being one among many others, but I am *the* sinner, having felt the personal conviction of my sin before God. The root meaning of the Greek word "sin" is "missing the mark." With all the blessings God has given me, I have missed the mark, the target, the purpose, for which He created me. As the chief of sinners, I desperately need God's mercy. We all do.

Pray for humbling grace, so that you might pray as a needy, unworthy suppliant to the great and holy God of the universe. Every cry of a broken heart to God is a *true* prayer. These are the prayers that God delights to hear.

PRAY BOLDLY

Let us therefore come boldly unto the throne of grace, that we may obtain mercy, and find grace to help in time of need.

—HEBREWS 4:16

If entering a palace, approaching a king, or addressing a monarch requires boldness, then certainly speaking to the King of kings requires boldness. Praying with a circumspect boldness is biblical.

We need proper vision to pray boldly. We must see who we are—sinners. We must see who God is—the perfectly holy and righteous King, before whom the angels cover their faces and cry, "Holy, holy, holy" (Isa. 6:3). How can the thought of approaching God produce boldness? Will it not produce humility instead? It is important to realize that genuine humility and genuine boldness are not opposites. The publican's prayer was truly humble. Smiting his chest, standing with bowed head, he viewed himself as the sinner. Yet, he came; he entered the King's house; he prayed to God. He was truly bold. As a bold beggar, he was compelled to enter the King's dwelling. He dared to speak to the King!

On what basis can a poor, sin-polluted beggar find the boldness needed to approach God's throne? Only by realizing that the King's throne is a "throne of grace." The beggar dares to approach because the King delights in mercy, in showing love to the miserable. He dares, because the King delights in grace, in showing love to the undeserving.

Grace and mercy testify of Jesus Christ. Jesus Christ embodies and personifies God's willingness to be reconciled with sinners and to show goodwill toward men. Christ unveils God's tender heart in His loving invitations: "Come unto me, all ye that labour and are heavy laden" (Matt. 11:28); "though your sins be as scarlet" (Isa. 1:18); and "I have no pleasure in the death of the wicked" (Ezek. 33:11). Authentic boldness results from a right view of Christ and who God is through Him for lost sinners. The sinner sees, through Christ, something of the fatherly heart of God as a heart that burns with forgiving love for returning prodigals.

False boldness, or presumption, is the opposite. The Pharisee knows neither himself nor God. He believes that he can please God in his person and by his work. He sees no need for Christ's Person and work. False boldness lacks true humility.

Praying boldly is praying humbly. Knowledge of self and knowledge of God are truths in tandem. When a sinner sees himself, he is humbled. He has no rights, no possessions—he must beg. But when he views Christ, the One who invites the needy, the One who loves to feed and clothe beggars, he is encouraged to knock. Then he sees that, for Christ's sake, God's throne is a throne of grace and that he is still living in the time of grace.

If an Old Testament Israelite had gone to the tabernacle to appear before God without a priest or mediator, he would have been too fearful to do so. God does not accept fruits from our own field, like Cain's. But the Israelites knew that a priest was there to offer sacrifices and to approach God on their behalf.

Here lies the heartbeat of boldness. Christ, as our High Priest, provides freedom and boldness to approach God. You may tremble when approaching the King, as Esther did in her approach to Ahasuerus, but has there ever been one trembling sinner to whom Jesus Christ did not hold out His golden scepter? No, never! Through Christ's mercy, at His throne of grace, a sinner finds true boldness.

You need humble boldness—humility when viewing your sinful self and boldness when viewing a reconciling Christ. Boldness without humility and humility without boldness are both sinful. Both deny the God of Scripture. Both do not believe that God is who He says He is. The one denies His justice, the other ignores His mercy. Both reveal unbelief. May God enable you to pray both humbly, as a sinner, and boldly, as one who trusts in Christ.

PRAY WAITING UPON GOD ⓼

And Elijah said unto Ahab, Get thee up, eat and drink; for there is a sound of abundance of rain. So Ahab went up to eat and to drink. And Elijah went up to the top of Carmel; and he cast himself down upon the earth, and put his face between his knees, and said to his servant, Go up now, look toward the sea. And he went up, and looked, and said, There is nothing. And he said, Go again seven times. And it came to pass at the seventh time, that he said, Behold, there ariseth a little cloud out of the sea, like a man's hand. And he said, Go up, say unto Ahab, Prepare thy chariot, and get thee down, that the rain stop thee not. And it came to pass in the mean while, that the heaven was black with clouds and wind, and there was a great rain. And Ahab rode, and went to Jezreel. And the hand of the LORD was on Elijah; and he girded up his loins, and ran before Ahab to the entrance of Jezreel.

—1 KINGS 18:41–46

The previous scene on Mt. Carmel was one of remarkable power—God answered Elijah's prayer by fire and all the priests of Baal were killed. After such success, Elijah does not wait for applause or fame. His ear is more spiritually attuned. He listens for another sound—"a sound of abundance of rain." He is alone, head between his knees, bowing in expectant prayer before God. He prays with his ears open, listening for the expected rain, and with his eyes watching for it.

To "wait on" or "wait upon" the Lord are common biblical phrases, occurring twenty-one times in the Old Testament. The root of the Hebrew word translated "wait on" means "to wait expectantly." It is the same Hebrew word used to describe a servant's attitude toward his master, always watching, expecting motions or looks to direct his service (Ps. 123:2).

Examine your own prayer life. Are you praying expectantly? Is your faith focused upward, looking for the "clouds" that contain God's answer? Or do the sights and sounds of people absorb your focus and concentration? After pouring out his soul and pleading for rain, Elijah instructs his servant, "Go up now, look toward the sea." Elijah's praying is expectant, for he was trusting in God's promise (1 Kings 17). Lack of expectation can be a serious fault in our prayers; we pray but do not go to a vantage point from which we can "look toward the sea" for the fulfilment of God's promises.

If we are truly waiting *for* God, we will also be waiting *upon* Him. For example, this morning when you read your Bible, was your mind's eye upon the Master? Were you asking, "Is there spiritual food here for me?" Did you read the Scriptures expectantly, asking, "What divine instruction is there here for me?" When attending church, do you ask, "What truth will the Lord apply to my heart?" Do you remember the Canaanite woman who continued looking to the Lord, expectantly waiting upon the words and actions of Christ (Matt. 15:21–28)? This is what Scripture calls us to.

Expectant prayer conquers discouragement. There are times when we pray and do not see an answer: there is not a single cloud in the sky, not the trace of an answer. At such times, we can conclude that our prayer is in vain; God will not answer it at all. Expectant prayer, however, looks beyond the cloudless skies. It views God, looking for His clouds and listening for His approaching footsteps. Expectant prayer goes again to pray and to look — seven times or more, if necessary.

Waiting upon the Lord is the opposite of a fatalistic and self-excusing spirit. This deadly attitude complains, "I can do nothing; what will be, will be." Rather, waiting upon God is active, intense, careful, personal, expectant waiting. Psalm 27:14 tells us to "Wait on the LORD: be of good courage, and he shall strengthen thine heart: wait, I say, on the LORD." The capitalized name of the Lord indicates Jehovah (Yahweh), the faithful, unchanging, covenant-keeping God, the eternal "I am that I am." This is the hope that enables us to wait expectantly, going to look again and again for the Lord's answer. Unexpectant prayer does not even look for God's answer. Wavering prayer may only look two or three times, being quickly discouraged by a cloudless sky. Such prayers lack the expectant attitude of believers who look "seven times." Those praying expectantly pray and pray, looking again and again.

Waiting upon God is an exercise of faith, hope, and love, especially in times of adversities, trials, and setbacks. Having faith in God means not looking to self, not having faith in self, but instead looking expectantly to God. We must look to Him, not to ourselves. We may not be able to see the solution to our problems; circumstances may be dark and confusing, but we continue to wait upon the Lord, for He is our King (Ps. 20:9). Wait upon God with anticipation and expectation. Look forward to His help and care.

God often exercises and strengthens our faith, hope, and love immeasurably through active waiting. The seventh time Elijah's servant looked, he said, "There ariseth a little cloud out of the sea, like a man's hand." This sign is all that expectant faith needs; by faith Elijah sees the rain already and instructs Ahab to go down, that "the rain stop thee not." Unexpectant prayer has Thomas's attitude: "Elijah, I will not believe it until the drops fall. A cloud is not rain. I must first see it and then I will believe." But Elijah sees fulfillment in the little cloud on the horizon.

And then, Elijah runs. He runs before the king's chariot all the way to Jezreel, full of expectancy in God. God instructs us to pray expectantly, waiting on Him.

What a wonderful privilege it is during setbacks and trials to walk and run by grace with hope, waiting on the Almighty! Then we experience an inward calm in unsettling circumstances, light in darkness, and sing praise to God while bound in the dungeon. This is only possible through Jesus Christ who merited the grace of holy waiting through His sufferings. He applies His own Word: "Wait on the LORD: be of good courage, and he shall strengthen thine heart: wait, I say, on the LORD" (Ps. 27:14).

PRAY INTERCEDINGLY

And Miriam and Aaron spake against Moses because of the Ethiopian woman whom he had married: for he had married an Ethiopian woman. And they said, Hath the LORD indeed spoken only by Moses? hath he not spoken also by us? And the LORD heard it.... And the cloud departed from off the tabernacle; and, behold, Miriam became leprous, white as snow: and Aaron looked upon Miriam, and, behold, she was leprous.... And Moses cried unto the Lord, saying, Heal her now, O God, I beseech thee.

—NUMBERS 12:1–2, 10, 13

God's law, in one word, requires love. The first table of the law requires love to God, the second, love to others. This other-oriented love must be evident in our prayers. By nature, we are self-centered. Self, as a clear testimony of our sinful rebellion, is our god. Selfishness sticks to us like glue; it even permeates our prayers. Test yourself today: In your personal prayers, for whom did you pray? How much time did you devote to the needs of others compared to your own? Were you praying for the spiritual needs of others this morning? How much time was devoted to praying for your family, fellow church members, office-bearers, teachers, students, governing officials, and neighbors?

How much time today did you devote to prayer for those with whom you are encountering difficulties? Did you pray more for yourself, for help in handling difficult situations, or did you truly pray for others? How much time did you devote to praying for those with special needs, cares, and concerns? If we truly love others, we love to pray for others. This does not mean that it is wrong to pray for ourselves, which is an important responsibility. But it is not our only responsibility. It is not wrong to care for ourselves—for our spiritual, emotional, mental, and physical needs—but the key to maintaining a proper balance in prayer is obeying the Scripture's command that we must love others as ourselves.

The value of intercessory prayer is tremendous. So often we view those leading the forces of God against the enemies, like Moses, as the most important people serving the church. We forget the value of the "Aarons" and "Hurs" who are holding up the blessing hands in prayer (Ex. 17:12). If the Aarons and the Hurs tire, Moses' hands droop, and the church gains and accomplishes nothing. Who is serving the church most today? It may well be its intercessors, whom few would know by name.

We need to distinguish between public service and private service in the church of God. God has given abilities for both, and both are important. We need leaders like Moses, but we also need supporters like Aaron and Hur. Victory requires both. God has called and ordained men to serve publicly in His church. But He also calls "mothers in Israel" to serve privately with intercessory prayers and often blesses women with tender, prayerful hearts for others.

Praying for others and loving others are inseparable graces. Do you have enemies? Pray daily, sincerely, and earnestly for them. Those who pray in this manner will discover that they cannot view their former enemies as enemies anymore. Hatred disappears. This is one of the most beautiful fruits of intercessory prayer. You cannot hate a person for whom you are truly praying.

In Numbers 12 we witness Aaron and Miriam's jealousy of Moses' position. Moses was innocent of wrongdoing but they started finding fault with him behind his back, calling attention to his marriage to a non-Israelite, Ethiopian woman. In addition, they claimed that God had also spoken through them; Moses, they scoffed, was not so special. These accusations and claims implied that Moses was pushing himself to the foreground. Aaron and Miriam publicly undermined Moses' divine calling and position.

What would your reaction be if you discovered that another person was unjustly criticizing your decisions or choices, questioning your motives, and attacking you behind your back?

When God struck Miriam with leprosy, what did Moses do? Did he say, "That's good! That's what she deserves after treating me the way she did"? Did he say, "Let her remain leprous for a while, that she may learn a lesson and be a good example for others"? No. By God's grace, he responded with intercessory prayer: "And Moses cried unto the LORD, saying, Heal her now, O God, I beseech thee" (v. 13). Would your reaction be similar to Moses'? Would you have done as Moses did?

Scripture provides us with an example of intercessory prayer that exceeds even that of Moses: the Example of examples, Jesus Christ. After His tormentors pounded the nails into His hands, He prayed, "Father, forgive them"

(Luke 23:34). Even now, in heaven, Christ continually intercedes for His people's security, assurance, and comfort. All of His people are carried on His High Priestly shoulders and are bound upon His High Priestly heart. May this be the pattern for us to follow, so that we too may have the needs of others bound upon our hearts and addressed in our prayers.

And, behold, a woman of Canaan came out of the same coasts, and cried unto him, saying, Have mercy on me, O Lord, thou Son of David; my daughter is grievously vexed with a devil. But he answered her not a word. And his disciples came and besought him, saying, Send her away; for she crieth after us. But he answered and said, I am not sent but unto the lost sheep of the house of Israel. Then came she and worshipped him, saying, Lord, help me. But he answered and said, It is not meet to take the children's bread, and to cast it to dogs. And she said, Truth, Lord; yet the dogs eat of the crumbs which fall from their masters' table. Then Jesus answered and said unto her, O woman, great is thy faith; be it unto thee even as thou wilt. And her daughter was made whole from that very hour.

—MATTHEW 15:21–28

There is a significant difference between an offered prayer and an answered prayer. Often, between our prayer and God's answer there are important spiritual lessons for us to learn. How often we can be full of sinful doubting and distrusting of the Lord through our ignorance of His ways! How often we reason, "I pray but God does not hear me," when, in reality, we do not hear God's silent message to us. God has heard our prayers, but we, proud creatures, rebel against His sovereignty. Instead, we desire to be sovereign. We think that our prayers should be answered how, when, and where we want.

The Lord Jesus heard the cry of the Canaanitish woman (Matt. 15:22), but did not answer her right away (v. 23). Many times we are so slow to understand God's answer, especially when He answers through silence. Why does the Lord do this? Often when we pray, we think that God should grant us our requests because we are worthy to be heard or because we are sincere. We think that God is obliged to hear us. But the Lord answers by giving no answer. The Canaanitish woman had to experience that she had no right to be heard—even her perseverance in prayer gave her no claim before God. What did she do when she experienced God's silence and realized that God was not immediately granting her request? Did she say that praying was meaningless? Did she abandon praying? No, she persevered all the more. She cried after Him all the louder, until even the disciples asked Jesus to send her away (v. 23).

Jesus answers His disciples, "I am not sent but unto the lost sheep of the house of Israel" (v. 24). By doing this, He is speaking indirectly to the Canaanitish woman. She is an outsider; she is not one of the chosen house of Israel. Have you ever been convinced that you are a sinful outsider? Have you struggled internally with such thoughts as, "There would be hope if I were one of the elect, but I am an outsider!" This was not Satan speaking to the Canaanitish woman, but Christ! He still had not answered her directly, but had only spoken to her indirectly by speaking to His disciples. It seems as though she is not worthy for Him to address directly. Perhaps we would say to her, "Give up. Go back home. Can't you see by now that Jesus is not interested in helping you?" But no, she perseveres. She finds hope even in this apparent rejection, for Jesus had noticed her. Therefore, she pleads, "Lord, help me."

Finally, Jesus answers her directly (v. 26). But what a discouraging answer! It is as though He says, "You are not one of My children, but a dog. It is not right to take the bread of My children and to give it to dogs. It would not be right or just for Me to help you. You are not worthy of it." Now she will give up, right? She just heard an apparent rejection from His own mouth! Yet she finds hope in this seemingly hopeless answer, for He has now spoken to her. She perseveres.

So far, the Canaanite woman received three answers to her persevering prayer: 1. silence; 2. that mercy was not for "outsiders," but only for the children of Israel; 3. that it would not be right to give the children's bread to "dogs."

Are not all these answers very discouraging? Are not all these "answers to prayer" against her? While it may appear so, yet all these "answers" were for her—to bring her empty-handed at the Savior's feet and to strip away all her rights and claims. Through this process, she learned to hang, plead, and depend solely on Christ's mercy—to persevere in prayer.

Jesus told her that it was not right to give the children's portion to dogs. She responded, "Truth, Lord: yet the dogs eat of the crumbs which fall from their masters' table." She perseveres by asking, as it were, "Are not the dogs allowed to eat the crumbs that fall from the table? I ask, Lord, only for a crumb! Grant me a dog's portion." This is persevering in prayer. Persevering prayer does not give up. Like the beggar who places his foot in the door so that it cannot be closed, so is the one who will not and cannot stop praying for an answer.

Christ's answer commends her faith — it takes faith to persevere, and great faith to persevere as she did. Do you perceive Christ's wisdom in His first three answers? If He had given her His fourth answer immediately, she may have left thinking she was worthy, or that her prayers were worthy, or that God was bound to grant her request. But now, she receives an answer through which she rejoices completely in the free grace of God in Jesus Christ (v. 28).

This incident is a great encouragement to us to persevere in prayer. It would appear that God was pushing this Canaanite woman away and keeping her at a distance. With His left hand He seems to not answer and to discourage her, but with His right hand He secretly draws her closer to Himself. He was emptying her of her self-worth and merit with His first three answers, only to fill her with *His* worth and merit — His rich, free, and sovereign grace — in the fourth answer.

Pray perseveringly. Persevere even when it seems you are regressing. Say with David, "I had fainted, unless I had believed to see the goodness of the LORD in the land of the living. Wait on the LORD: be of good courage, and he shall strengthen thine heart: wait, I say, on the LORD" (Ps. 27:13–14).

PRAY THANKFULLY

O give thanks unto the LORD; for he is good; for his mercy endureth for ever.
—PSALM 136:1

It is everyone's duty to give thanks to God. Being thankful to God is to acknowledge that He has acted graciously toward us. This is not a requirement only for those exercised at deeper levels in their prayer life, or only for established Christians. God requires thankfulness from everyone. "In every thing by prayer and supplication with thanksgiving let your requests be made known unto God" (Phil. 4:6).

First, we are to be thankful for mercies received—"our creation, preservation, and all the blessings of this life" (Belgic Confession of Faith). We are not only to be thankful when we receive remarkably clear answers to prayer. We are also to be thankful for the things we receive for which we did not ask. Imagine making a list of all the times we used our senses, physical strength, and mental abilities in one day. Think of the simple act of eating a slice of bread, of receiving the strength and muscle coordination to lift our hand, to chew, and to digest it. Perhaps we never specifically asked God for these blessings or for thousands of others today, but God graciously gave them to us anyway.

Second, we are to be thankful for trials endured. We must not only be thankful for clear answers to prayer and for blessings for which we did not pray, but our thankfulness must penetrate deeper: we are called also to be thankful for trials and tests (James 1:2), for those things that distress us, events that are not pleasant or comfortable or to our liking. Paul and Silas sang psalms in the inner prison—songs of praise to God when they had bleeding backs and shackled feet.

Those of us who are adults can visualize this truth by picturing our earthly fathers. Is it not true that when we were younger we hated our dads' punishments, chastisements, and training? Sometimes we even became angry or rebellious. Now, however, we can look back and say, "Thank you, Dad, for the training you gave me, for guiding and disciplining me in the way I should go. I did not understand it at the time, but now I see its value."

The subject of thankfulness highlights a common sore spot in prayer. We can pray thinking of the Lord as a "limited God," not an "all-encompassing God." What is the difference between an emergency phone number and that of a friend? The one you call only when you must, when you have no choice, only in times of emergency. But the other you *love* to call—when things are going well as well as when things are going badly.

Think of the ten lepers healed by Christ. Nine used the "emergency number" for God because they only wanted to be healed. But only one used the number of a friend. He returned to Christ, with a heart full of love, communion, and praise. The joy that exceeded the priest's pronouncement that he was clean was the joy of his heart being full of love for Jesus Christ.

There is a difference between joy and thankfulness. Joy focuses more upon the blessings, but thankfulness focuses on the One who blesses. Scripture teaches us to count God's blessings, as the old hymn states, to "name them one by one." We are more prone to count our blessings by hundreds and to give thanks in bundles. In our busyness, we often ignore or trample on the God-given grass and lilies of the field! We rarely pause to see a flower's beauty, or smell its fragrance. How many "flowers" in your life have you passed by, never noticing the love and beauty with which God clothed each one of them? Do we pause to thank God for His "flowers" petal by petal?

We are so prone to count our one or two troubles and so quick to dwell upon that one unkind word more than upon another hundred kind words for which we should be so deeply thankful. True thankfulness brings us close to the heart of God, to His love and grace. True thankfulness realizes that anything short of hell is grace. True thankfulness serves as a corrective lens—a lens through which we see God's grace in all things. Have you ever seen a severely sick person who is deeply thankful for the care he receives? A very old, physically frail person who is deeply thankful that she has a clear mind? Or a dying person who is deeply thankful that he still has time to speak to his family? Such a person has learned something of the art of thankfulness.

Third, we are to be thankful for the absolute goodness and infinite mercy of God expressed in His actions toward us in both prosperity and adversity. "O give thanks unto the LORD; *for he is good*: for his mercy *endureth forever.*" We must give thanks for who God is, in all His dealings with us. To do this, we must understand something of who we are in relation to who God is. Then we begin to realize why this expression is repeated twenty-six times in Psalm 136! Does it also resound anew each day in your life? Is not our God a wonderful God? When you look back in your life, do you see that His mercy really does endure forever? Looking around you, do you observe that His mercy is surrounding you on every side? Does this not make your sin the more terrible and repulsive? How often are we guilty of not thanking the Lord, of ignoring and insulting Him?

Prayer is the chief part of thankfulness. Is thanking and praising God your heart's desire, whether in adversity or prosperity? There is no greater blessing than receiving a truly thankful heart from God, and no greater joy than pouring out your heart to Him in thankful prayer. Pray thankfully.

WRESTLING IN PRAYER 12

*For we wrestle not against flesh and blood, but against prin-
cipalities, against powers, against the rulers of the darkness of
this world, against spiritual wickedness in high places.*
—EPHESIANS 6:12

When praying, we must wrestle with Satan and with our
sinful nature. We wrestle with Satan who tries to block us
from spiritual life or, if we have received it, to hinder our
spiritual growth. Satan continually strives to find the most
effective ways to keep us from prayer. Our sinful nature is
Satan's ally. It is filled with enmity against God. By nature,
we try to be gods to ourselves—to handle our lives in our
own way.

Because enemies lurk without and within, you should
not be surprised when you find it difficult to pray. Our bod-
ies, minds, and hearts naturally oppose it. That is why we
are called to wrestle in prayer. Wrestling involves combat,
strategy, focus, and determination.

In the first place, you need to designate a time and place
to be alone with God. You must fight to do that. There are
so many pressing things to do: work to be finished, children
to care for, meetings to attend, projects to complete. To set

our priorities correctly requires wrestling; it needs God's all-conquering grace to establish the priority of prayer.

Secondly, when we are alone with God for prayer, at a set place and time, the wrestling is far from over. Our attempts to pray can be so bombarded with other thoughts—thoughts about the activities of the day, the problems we must deal with, the people we must meet, or the tasks we must complete. We must wrestle to focus our thoughts upon God in prayer. We can spend many ten-minute prayer sessions reviewing past experiences and events, imagining how we will deal with future events. Restlessly, we bounce upon the waves of uncertain self, adrift on a sea of self-reliance. Prayer is not a spiritual rest, however, unless we focus upon the Almighty, the One who lives and reigns over all, the One who quiets the winds and waves with a word. True prayer wars to find, focus upon, and take hold of God in Christ. Wrestlings in prayer are to bring our hearts into harmony with the spirit of prayer.

Your prayer time is an appointment with the Great Physician. But as prayer patients, we are often amazingly foolish. Imagine for a moment, a person with deep chest pain who secures an appointment with his doctor. He tells the physician at great length about all his symptoms and pain, his fears of what this may lead to, his ideas on how to cure it, and then stands up and leaves. Would this patient not be a foolish one? When we go to a physician, we expect to be examined. We willingly submit to that for our own good, combating the urge to leave and go somewhere more comfortable. We expect a diagnosis and desire a prescription. And we faithfully take the prescribed medicine, even if it is bitter to our taste.

In how many prayer "appointments" have we failed to listen to the heavenly Physician? Great wrestling is required to open our hearts and submit to His examination. Our doctors and dentists often use a strong light to aid in their examinations. If the light of the Holy Spirit focuses upon us, by nature we squirm. If He examines our motives, we try to hide from His scrutiny. We keep our hoarded money under the cover of "thriftiness"; we hide our lack of concern and care for others behind a "full schedule"; we conceal our dislike and hatred of others under "the wrong things they have done to me." When divine light focuses on us, we wrestle with ourselves to submit quietly to its examination.

But we cannot do this in our own strength. Jacob-like, we need our thighs to be put out of joint so we cry, "Lord bless me for I cannot prosper without this; I cannot let Thee go until Thou dost bless me" (cf. Gen. 32:24–32). Our wrestling to pray and struggling in prayer must be "in the Spirit" (Eph. 6:18). Jeremiah asked, "Is there no balm in Gilead; is there no physician there? why then is not the health of the daughter of my people recovered?" (Jer. 8:22). Could the answer be that we wrestle too much to assert our own diagnosis and prescriptions, rather than receiving the heavenly Physician's? Jacob-like, we must also have our names changed—from "self-helper" to "God-seeker." Wrestle in prayer.

13

WAITING FOR ANSWERS TO PRAYER

Therefore his sisters sent unto him, saying, Lord, behold, he whom thou lovest is sick. Then said Martha unto Jesus, Lord, if thou hadst been here, my brother had not died. When Jesus therefore saw her weeping, and the Jews also weeping which came with her, he groaned in the spirit, and was troubled, and said, Where have ye laid him? They said unto him, Lord, come and see.
—JOHN 11:3, 21, 33–34

God often seems to delay answers to prayer. The Lord promised Abraham that his seed would be as the stars of the heaven—innumerable. But Abraham was still childless at seventy-five years of age when he entered the land of Canaan; Isaac was not born until Abraham was a hundred years old. God promised David that he would be king of Israel, but for years he fled from Saul, hunted as a fugitive. During this delayed time, David became so discouraged that he cried, "One day I shall perish at the hands of Saul" (1 Sam. 27:1). Elizabeth was so old that Zacharias did not believe the angel's promise of a son. And Martha and Mary chided the Lord in their grief—if He had come sooner, they complained, Lazarus would not have died and all this grief would not have happened.

We read in Habakkuk 2:3, "...*though it tarry,* wait for it; because it will surely come, it *will not tarry*" (emphasis added). This verse appears to contradict itself, but it does not. Think of it as referring to two different clocks. One clock is our perspective and time; the other is God's. Our perspective refers to delays, tarryings, and waitings. We want answers now, when *we* think we need it. We do not want to wait. God's perspective, however, sees the most opportune time. He will not tarry one moment beyond the fullness of time—the *best* time to answer. David had learned this truth when he asked God to answer his prayer "in an acceptable time"—whenever the Lord knew was best (Ps. 69:13b). Hence the psalmist could confess: "God is our refuge and strength, a very present help in trouble" (Ps. 46:1).

We may call God's time a delay, but this is due to our limited perspective and understanding. Would Abraham and Sarah have viewed Isaac as a gift from God to the same degree if he had been conceived decades earlier? Would John the Baptist's birth be understood as a miracle? Would an immediate answer to Mary and Martha's prayer have best promoted God's glory? In this example from John 11, Martha and Mary could not understand the Lord Jesus' silence and delay. Why did He act in this way? Why did He not answer? Why did He permit the enemy to conquer? Why did He permit all this evil, sorrow, and turmoil to occur?

Why? Because often God's way is to kill in order to make alive, so that He may be glorified (John 11:4). He brought life out of barren wombs and sealed tombs. He brought light from darkness. He works through impossibilities in order to raise to life our dead hopes. It is God who brings dead hopes to life, working through impossibilities to display and glorify His own work. Zacharias and Elisabeth, Abraham and Sarah could clearly perceive that their children were God's miraculous gifts; David would clearly realize that his ascension to the throne was not his own doing; Mary and Martha glorified God all the more when they understood that Jesus did not delay, but came at the opportune time so that a greater miracle could occur. When Christ raised Lazarus, the people spoke of God's glorious deeds.

God's timing is perfect. We must learn to see that God's timing transcends ours. He does not delay; His time is the best time. Seeing "delays" reflects that we are trusting too much in our judgments—using our "time" as the standard by which to measure God's actions. We must learn that *He* is God, not *we*. Learn to pray with your eye on God's clock, not yours.

14

PRAY WITH APPETITE

Open thy mouth wide, and I will fill it.
—PSALM 81:10

Our prayer life is an indicator of our spiritual appetite. We must examine ourselves to see what size servings of spiritual food satisfy us. Are some of us, who are true children of the living God, surviving on portions so scanty that we can barely stay alive? How lean our personal prayers and devotions can be! For those of us living in this way there seems to be so little for which we need God. There appears to be so little to confess to Him, so little for which to thank Him. Is it any wonder then, if we have little or no spiritual strength, but easily faint on the way?

When Joash was called to Elisha's bedside, the prophet commanded him to smite the ground with his arrows. He smote three times and stopped. He thought, "That's enough." But Elisha reprimanded him, saying, "Thou shouldest have smitten five or six times; then hadst thou smitten Syria till thou hadst consumed it" (2 Kings 13:19).

So it can be with prayer. You can say, "I prayed; I opened my mouth," but God's loving command is not merely "Open thy mouth," but "Open thy mouth *wide*." True believers are not to sip only a little milk, but they are to drink a full glass. Life speaks of growth. Healthy spiritual life also grows; it matures. We must learn to eat stronger spiritual meat, to grow in grace. How often James's words are sadly fulfilled, even in the lives of God's children: "Ye have not, because ye ask not" (James 4:2). God does not hinder us and there is no limit to Christ's fullness; we hinder and limit ourselves.

When you woke up this morning, how fully aware were you of your need for God? Did you walk fully with God "in the cool of the day" through today's anticipated needs? Were you fully aware and conscious of your sins and your blessings? Did you experience a full need for a full God for a full day?

Would you, as a parent, ignore your child who was crying with hunger if you had food to feed him? Do you then think that if *you* cry to God for bread, that *He* will give you a stone? Are you more gracious than God? Unbelief refuses to trust that God is who He says He is and will do as He has promised. Unbelief questions the love and doubts the faithfulness of our God and Savior.

God's grace is full and free. He says, "Open thy mouth wide, and I *will* fill it." He does not say "maybe" but "I *will*." Let God be true and every other voice, especially the inner voice of unbelief, be a liar! God's grace is wide as the ocean. He is the supply for the widow's never-emptying jug of oil. Every vessel that her sons brought she filled to overflowing. God commands us to exercise our faith—"open thy mouth *wide*." The amount of jars collected represented the amount of faith exercised; God was willing to fill all that were collected. The oil stopped flowing only when there were no more vessels to fill (2 Kings 4:1–7).

God gives food to the hungry. What a blessing to experience a daily, growing, healthy, spiritual appetite! All such
hungering souls shall be filled. "Open thy mouth wide, and
I will fill it," says the Lord. Pray with appetite for the Lord's
fullness. Dare to ask for all that God has promised.

15

PRAY FOR LABORERS

*Then saith he unto his disciples, The harvest truly is plente-
ous, but the labourers are few; pray ye therefore the Lord of
the harvest, that he will send forth labourers into his harvest.*
— MATTHEW 9:37–38

Prayer is an important work in the kingdom of God. We are
commanded to pray for the gifts that are needed in the Lord's
work. We often hear people say, "We need more ministers."
We do, but many times we are afraid that we are talking to
the wrong person—we say it to other people instead of the
Sender. Are we praying for more ministers, elders, deacons,
missionaries, and for more church members who actively
reach out to minister to others?

Many stop at the first part of our text, "The harvest truly
is plenteous, but the labourers are few." They stop before
Christ stops. Christ continues: "Pray ye therefore...."

We must ask for this gift; it is to be *prayed* for. It is not my
or your prayers that will send forth active workers. *Christ*
will send forth laborers. He sends; we do not. The Lord
calls us to make active use of His means and the primary
means mentioned here is prayer—praying for gifts to meet
kingdom needs. "The effectual fervent prayer of a righteous

man availeth much" (James 5:16b). "This is the confidence that we have in him, that, if we ask any thing according to his will, he heareth us" (1 John 5:14).

Do you feel the need for the gifts of scriptural understanding, experience, vision, leadership, teaching, and outreach? Are we praying for these gifts, pleading God's promise, "If ye then, being evil, know how to give good gifts unto your children: how much more shall your heavenly Father give the Holy Spirit to them that ask him" (Luke 11:13)?

Our verse instructs us, "Pray *ye* therefore (because you see the need) the Lord of the harvest, that he *will* send forth labourers into his harvest" (emphasis added). Christ's own words show that He will send forth laborers in answer to our prayers. Consequently, all believers are to be praying for this.

The book of Judges witnesses to the truth of this text. For years there was no judge in Israel and as the need became more pressing, the people turned to God in prayer. The Lord allowed the people to entreat Him when they prayed for a new judge to lead them into battle. Oh, that every church member would be active in prayer with our need for church leaders and workers—not to send them forth in our own strength or choosing, but to pray that *Christ* will send them forth!

But we are not only commanded to pray for receiving the gifts of having leaders, but also to pray for gifts of leadership to be bestowed upon our leaders. Leading is difficult, strenuous work. When it looks like everything is in order to march forward in ranks, there are unexpected problems, like the attacks from behind that the Amalekites instigated against Moses and Israel. The church needs "Aarons" and "Hurs" to pray for the gifts of strength, courage, wisdom, vision, love, and grace that leaders need (Ex. 17:12). God's plan is so beautiful, in which His body, the church, prays to its Head, Jesus Christ, for its care and health. The health and extension of the church is bound upon the heart of the Savior. In such prayers, the heart and will of God and His church are one. May the Lord richly bless us with a gift-needing spirit and gift-praying grace. Pray with vision for the needs of God's kingdom; pray for laborers to gather in the promised harvest.

16

PRAY WATCHFULLY

Watch and pray, that ye enter not into temptation: the spirit indeed is willing, but the flesh is weak. —MATTHEW 26:41

The Lord commands us to watch and pray. The Greek word for "watch" speaks of guarding. Soldiers on guard duty were said to be "on watch." The history of Nehemiah and the Jews beautifully illustrates this, when they carried both sword and trowel while rebuilding Jerusalem's wall. They not only had to build, but they also had to be on watch because the enemy was always near. This example pictures our duty. In every sphere of our lives God calls us to build and to watch. God calls us to serve as workmen with both the sword and trowel. This is also true regarding prayer life. As we seek grace to pray, we must be on "watch," we must be on guard. We must watch against distractions, temptations, and the weakness of our own flesh. We must guard against wandering, self-centered thoughts and all types of foolish imaginations.

When we enter into personal prayer, Satan goes on his guard. He is never more on guard, alert, and disturbed than when he sees a person at prayer. Satan knows that he can defeat any human being, but is powerless against the living

God to whom that person prays. Prayer is the critical point where true, practical religion begins. Prayer is where spiritual life flourishes, but also where it decays, for backsliding usually begins in our private prayers and then spreads to every area of our lives. Consequently, our prayer life can serve as a barometer of our spiritual life. It can serve as a predictor of future spiritual "weather," for it indicates our future direction. Small wonder, then, that we are commanded to pray watchfully.

What means has God blessed to help us pray watchfully? Some people find that preparing a list of concerns before they pray is helpful; others pray out loud to help them watch. Wandering thoughts and distracting cares are like the birds that kept coming down upon Abraham's sacrifice that he had to continually watch for and drive away (Gen. 15:11). The Lord Jesus commands that we watch and pray. Peter did not obey this instruction, and consider what it cost him.

We do not watch and pray by nature, left to ourselves. But there is One who did and who does this perfectly. He is the One whose prayers upheld Peter. He testified, "I have prayed for thee, [Peter], that thy faith fail not" (Luke 22:32). Jesus Christ is the perfect watchman on Zion's walls. He is the perfect praying High Priest. He is the greater Nehemiah, who perfectly builds the walls of Zion and perfectly guards His people as well. What encouragement this can be to us when we are discouraged with our own poor watching and praying! Salvation centers upon Jesus Christ—not upon us.

Sometimes God's children can see so many strong enemies and feel so surrounded that victory seems impossible and defeat seems certain. At such times, perhaps you feel ready to give up; your hands hang down. You look more at your weakness and your enemies' strength than to your God. Watching and praying is hard work. It involves internal struggles, battles, and combat against your own flesh, thoughts, and fears. It is a war against the old nature of sin and unbelief. Yet God has promised to uphold you in this warfare, so He lovingly commands, "Pray watchfully."

17

PRAY SINCERELY

The LORD is nigh unto all them that call upon him, to all that call upon him in truth.
— PSALM 145:18

In daily life, our hearts and tongues, words and works, prayers and practices need to echo one another. In our prayers, God does not note the expressiveness of our voice, the multitude of our words, or regard the eloquence of our expressions. Rather, He observes the sincerity of our heart. To pray sincerely is to pray without pretense or deceit. It is to be honest and frank with God in prayer, so that nothing is assumed or put on to impress Him.

God is looking for truth in the inward parts. There is a story of a slave boy who frequently heard his master's prayers, which never included the slaves. But the boy prayed, "God, give me a prayer to pray." Soon after, he overheard a Bible-reading about the Pharisee and the publican. When he heard the prayer of the Pharisee, he thought, "I could never pray a prayer like that. That man is far too good for me." But when he heard the simple prayer of the publican, "God be merciful to me a sinner," he thought, "That is a prayer for me. That is what I am; that is what I need."

Praying sincerely does not mean that we first attain a certain degree of sincerity and then pray. A sincere person knows and feels his imperfections; he deeply recognizes that his sincerity is not sincere enough. If we needed to become truly sincere in order for God to hear us, nobody would be able to pray. But someone asks, "Is not sincerity a quality that the Holy Spirit must work in my heart before I can truly pray?" We must answer "yes" and "no" to this question: Yes, the Holy Spirit must open our spiritual eyes to see sincerely that we are not sincere enough. But, no, we are never to think of our sincerity as a qualifying factor that earns us a right to God's attention and answer. This would drag us back into a covenant of works, making us like pagans who think they must bring something in their hands to please their gods in order to be heard.

Praying sincerely is not a condition in which we know that we are sincere enough to please God, but the opposite. In praying, confessing, needing, and begging for that which we do not have or possess, we reveal sincerity. The sinner sincerely knows that he is not sincere enough — that he neither seeks nor serves God with the sincerity of heart and the devotion of which the Lord is worthy. Because a person sincerely knows that he is a sinner, he can sincerely ask, seek, and knock for needed mercy; he can sincerely pray, "God be merciful to me a sinner."

If, on the other hand, a person knew that he was sincere enough, he would not realize himself to be a totally lost sinner, neither would he totally rely upon God's mercy. He would place some value and trust in his sincerity rather than exclusively in free and sovereign grace. We seem to get entangled in such problematics when we are looking too much at ourselves instead of focusing on God and Christ. Consider this example. A person encouraged a beggar to beg at a king's palace. He observed that other beggars who asked there had received, that those who sought had found, and that those who knocked had the door opened to them. But the beggar hesitated; he doubted. He thought, "I can't do that. Look at my coat, it's not nearly good enough for the king. My face is dirty, my shoes are old, my hands are filthy. I cannot beg at the king's door. He doesn't know me well enough and I haven't served him sincerely enough." If the beggar holds to this way of thinking, in the end, he will be outside of the king's blessing forever. Why? Because he is focused more on his own unworthiness than on the king's graciousness; he trusts more in his own preparedness instead of the king's mercy.

How insulting it is to the free and sovereign grace of God, when we, too, trust more in our efforts and works than in God's mercy and grace! We sin in God's sight when we look more to the degree of sincerity of our requests than to the degree of sincerity in God to hear and answer *graciously.* It is an affront to God to doubt His grace. We need God's almighty Spirit to break our self-trust and instill God-trust. So go as a beggar: ask, seek, and knock for this. Pray looking not to your sincerity, but rather to God's. Pray sincerely.

18

PRAY BY THE SPIRIT

Likewise the Spirit also helpeth our infirmities: for we know not what we should pray for as we ought: but the Spirit itself maketh intercession for us with groanings which cannot be uttered.
—ROMANS 8:26

Setting a time for devotion and prayer is like raising the sail on a ship. It is the means to catch the movement of the Spirit in the same way that a sail catches the wind. But Christians often fall into two errors in prayer that a sailor would never commit in sailing.

First, imagine watching a person trying to sail when there is no wind. This person then tries to produce his own wind by blowing or fanning various objects. What would you observe? You would see no movement. The person would quickly become tired and discouraged, and would finally give up. His efforts would be useless. This person is foolish, for the entire sailing mechanism is set to catch an air current far greater than anything he can produce. Sailboats without motors are not made to run on their own power. They must receive their moving power from outside themselves — from the wind.

The same is true of prayer. We can begin with good intentions, firm decisions, and interesting devotions. We set aside a time to read and pray and we set sail. But it can happen that we do not move. We can then begin to work furiously trying to generate our own air current. We try to produce "the wind" of our best sincerities and intentions; we try our best meditation books, our favorite parts of Scripture, but we still do not move. We try to fill our sails with our favorite expressions and best feelings, but our sails remain limp. It all brings fatigue and discouragement. All our efforts are of no use. Yet, this experience may be very useful; it may teach an important lesson. If a person thinks that he can move his boat by his own powers, he would not raise a sail, would he? Raising the boat's sail confesses his need of another power—the power of the wind. Raising the sail is an action of dependency—a confession that we need the wind. Prayer also is a confession of our own infirmities and dependency. Our lack of self-power is not a hindrance to sailing; it is the very reason for hoisting the sail. Spiritually, because we know we cannot move ourselves, we need to raise the sail of prayer, to catch the wind, the movement of the Spirit. We are called to set the sail, to actively use God's means of grace, but only the Spirit can breathe wind into the sails and move the ship.

Happily the Spirit delights to blow upon the sails of our ship through His intercession. Consequently, when we find it difficult or even impossible to pray, because of our infirmity and ignorance, we can rely on the intercession of the Spirit. "Likewise the Spirit also helpeth our infirmities: for we know not what we should pray for as we ought: but the Spirit itself maketh intercession for us with groanings which cannot be uttered" (Rom. 8:26).

Second, when sailing, the wind is seldom the same. Often, when sailing, you cannot see clearly whether you are moving or not. In fact, if you look at the water it can look like you are going backward. But when checking your location again after a little time, you can see that you have traveled farther. So with true prayer, the Spirit can move a person imperceptibly. Not all movements of the Spirit are strong winds; most are gentle breezes. Why? Because gentle movements are valuable to those who feel the Spirit's workings. If there are times when the breezes and winds of deep desire, longings, and groanings fill the sails of your soul, is this a movement of yourself?

If the wind dies down for a time, what do true sailors do? They keep their sails up, trusting that the wind will blow in their direction again. The Holy Spirit is compared to the wind. The Lord Jesus taught, "The wind bloweth where it listeth, and thou hearest the sound thereof, but canst not tell whence it cometh, and whither it goeth: so is every one that is born of the Spirit" (John 3:8). Your expectation must not be in your own generating power or in your own spirituality. Pray with, by, and in the Holy Spirit. Seek His help, guidance, intercession, and sustaining strength in order to pray as you should.

19

PRAY AND WORK

And the man bowed down his head, and worshipped the LORD. And he said, Blessed be the LORD God of my master Abraham, who hath not left destitute my master of his mercy and his truth: I being in the way, the LORD led me to the house of my master's brethren. —GENESIS 24:26–27

Abraham prayed that God would direct his servant to the right wife for Isaac, but he also worked—he used the means of sending his servant out to seek for a wife for his son. Bartimaeus placed himself near the road where Jesus was passing by and there he prayed, crying out, "Jesus, thou son of David, have mercy on me" (Mark 10:47).

Let us imitate Abraham's servant and Bartimaeus—pray and work. *Ora* is the Latin word for "pray"; *labora* means "work." These are the two oars God calls us to use. We are instructed to use both of these oars under God's guidance and blessing. If we use only one without the other, our boat will go in circles. Paul and Apollos must plant, but God alone can grant the increase. May God grant us to be prayerful planters, active in prayer and active in labor. We must be willing to put our all into sowing the seed (*labora*), while remaining deeply conscious that we cannot make one seed sprout so that we also put our all into prayer (*ora*). *Ora* and *labora*.

God enables His people to work on their knees and with their hands, graciously rewarding the service and prayers poured out to Him. Like Abraham's servant, we must bow our heads and worship Him, saying, "Blessed be God who has not left us destitute of His mercy and truth; we being in the way—the way of prayer and work—the Lord richly blessed us." May God grant us clearness of vision to see both of our duties—to labor as faithful servants and to pray as needy beggars.

God's Word tells us that such prayerful workdays will be followed by true thanksgiving days. The Bible is full of promises of spiritual blessing to those who pray and work: "Cast thy bread upon the waters: for thou shalt find it after many days" (Eccl. 11:1). "For as the rain cometh down, and the snow from heaven, and returneth not thither, but watereth the earth, and maketh it bring forth and bud, that it may give seed to the sower, and bread to the eater; so shall my word be that goeth forth out of my mouth: it shall not return unto me void, but it shall accomplish that which I please, and it shall prosper in the thing whereto I sent it" (Isa. 55:10–11). "They that sow in tears shall reap in joy. He that goeth forth and weepeth, bearing precious seed, shall doubtless come again with rejoicing, bringing his sheaves with him" (Ps. 126:5–6).

When we realize that we are but servants, simply, and often poorly, doing our duties, then we will also want to proclaim with the psalmist, "Not unto us, O LORD, not unto us, but unto thy name give glory, for thy mercy, and for thy truth's sake" (Ps. 115:1). God blesses prayerful work—not because our efforts are worthy, but because He is gracious and His promise true. So work at praying and pray when working. Prayerfully work.

20

PRAY REVERENTLY

Be not rash with thy mouth, and let not thine heart be hasty to utter any thing before God: for God is in heaven, and thou upon earth: therefore let thy words be few.

—ECCLESIASTES 5:2

God is greatly to be feared in the assembly of the saints, and to be had in reverence of all them that are about him.

—PSALM 89:7

Wherefore we receiving a kingdom which cannot be moved, let us have grace, whereby we may serve God acceptably with reverence and godly fear.

—HEBREWS 12:28

When he prayed for Sodom, Abraham showed reverence in how he approached the Lord. He pleaded, "Behold now, I have taken upon me to speak unto the Lord, which am but dust and ashes" (Gen. 18:27). Reverently, Job confessed, "I have heard of thee by the hearing of the ear: but now mine eye seeth thee. Wherefore I abhor myself, and repent in dust and ashes" (Job 42:5–6). If the sinless angels in heaven cover their faces and cry out, "Holy, holy, holy," in God's presence, how can we, sinful creatures, ever dare approach Him? How can we who are sinful people ever seek God's holy presence in prayer? How can we ever pray intimately to a perfect God? The only answer to these questions lies in Jesus Christ. God remains God. He is the King of kings, the Lord of lords. He is the perfection of holiness. No sinner can ever approach His holy presence, apart from Christ. But through Christ, God adopts sinners as His children. Through Christ, God and sinners can commune.

Are you, though intimate with the Lord, praying reverently? You can test yourself in four ways. First, test yourself when praying in the presence of your family or friends. When you pray, can both of these traits be heard? Can your family and friends hear that you are speaking to the King of kings with reverence and humility? Can they also hear that you are speaking to a deeply loved Father in intimacy and confidence? Balance is crucial in prayer. We can draw near to God as believers because He is our Father, but with reverance and godly fear because our Father is Almighty God (Heb. 12:28). Second, your balance must fit the circumstances. Public prayer reflects more reverence and less intimacy than private prayer. Third, in family or public prayer, when you are praying with or for a group, prayer must be reverent, yet edifying. You must exalt God, but also pray for the people who are praying with you. You must make your requests and thanksgivings understandable to everyone there. Finally, true reverence produces humility, as it avoids pride. True reverence avoids casualness and carelessness in posture, language, and approach. A reverent intimacy avoids routineness and redundancy.

When we pray, it is crucial that we view both who is praying and to whom we are praying; who we are and who God is. May God teach us these inseparable truths. We are called to pray—to pray reverently.

21

PRAY FERVENTLY

And Jacob was left alone; and there wrestled a man with him until the breaking of the day. And when he saw that he prevailed not against him, he touched the hollow of his thigh; and the hollow of Jacob's thigh was out of joint, as he wrestled with him. And he said, Let me go, for the day breaketh. And he said, I will not let thee go, except thou bless me. And he said unto him, What is thy name? And he said, Jacob. And he said, Thy name shall be called no more Jacob, but Israel: for as a prince hast thou power with God and with men, and hast prevailed.

—GENESIS 32:24–28

Fervency in prayer can often be more man-centered than God-centered. As Jacob, we, too, can wrestle fervently and persistently, but too often we do it in our own strength. We can seek our strength in our own accomplishments, Scripture reading, fervency, sincerity, persistency, or love of God's truth. We, too, can wrestle with God, trusting in the "strength" of all the things that we have done for the Lord. We trust that all our accomplishments and perseverance will overpower God so that He must answer our prayer. It is so natural for our self-centered hearts to trust in our own strength and abilities, but all such wrestling is actually fighting against God.

God will not prevail with us when we trust in our own strength. He must first break our strength; He must touch the "hollow of our thigh" to put it out of joint. Human strength and power do not impress or please the Lord. We must experience God touching the "hollow of our thigh." We must experience that our strength to stand and fight is finished. Such experiences are painful for our fleshly pride but necessary for our spiritual growth. Then, like Jacob, we can only cling to the Lord and plead for His help and deliverance. When our strength is gone, we realize our need for God. When God does break our strength, we experience our own weakness. Humility, rather than pride, then prevails.

Only such God-dependent sinners will be God-exalting prayer warriors. Such needy ones will pray fervently—no longer fervently wrestling in their own strength, but now fervently clinging to Christ. Such clinging ones cannot let Him go except He bless them; it is a matter of life or death. This was the apostle Paul's experience: "For when I am weak, then am I strong" (2 Cor. 12:10). Like Jacob, when Paul had no strength to stand in himself, he prevailed through Christ. In Hosea 12:4 we read, "Yea, he had power over the angel, and prevailed: he wept, and made supplication unto him." Such weepers, supplicators, and clingers shall prevail. We are to pray fervently and persistently, not in our strength, but fervently needing Christ's strength; not relying on our prayers to Him, but needing His prayers for us, and not trusting our merits, but trusting Christ's. Such beggars who cling to God's free and one-sided grace cling so strongly to Christ that He "cannot" break loose, for it captures His heart. Never in the Word of God do you read of one such needy beggar from whom Christ broke loose. All such fervent, persistent seekers held Him until He blessed them.

Our difficulty in prayer is that so often we wrestle with a fervency that resembles Jacob, the deceiving clinger, more than Israel, the one whose fervent persistency, by grace, prevailed with God. Those who cling to God as Israel did—those who need His grace and cannot go on without it—will prevail as princes with the King of kings. Such have power with God for they take hold of His heart, His heart of free and sovereign grace. Strong, "Jacob-like" wrestlers get nowhere, even when they wrestle the entire night. But fervent, broken-legged, "Israel-like" beggars prevail, undaunted by injury or the approach of dawn.

Has the Almighty touched the hollow of your spiritual thigh? Let us pray with all our mind and heart, soul and strength—and in that warmth of conviction stirred in us by the Spirit and the Word of God. Pray fervently and persistently.

22

PRAY CONSTANTLY

Pray without ceasing.
—1 THESSALONIANS 5:17

What does Scripture mean when it tells us to pray without ceasing? In the first place, it means to pray persistently. The widow in Luke 18 persisted in asking the unjust judge to care for her case. How much more should we not persist with pleading before a gracious Judge? Second, we must be instant in prayer. To be instant in prayer means that prayer is urgent and pressing; it is near the surface in our lives. Each new need and event produces new prayer. Young children speak instantly to their parents. Every pain or joy creates a fervent desire to tell father or mother so that the child can hardly contain him or herself. A childlike spirit should fill our walk with God. One fruit of this will be being instant in prayer.

Years ago, several ministers were meeting in one of their homes. They were discussing this very verse—to "pray without ceasing" (1 Thess. 5:17). What does it mean? How can this be done? In the busyness of life how can a person pray continually, without stopping? After considerable discussion and disagreement, they appointed a few members to study this matter and report back at next month's meeting. A young maid serving the ministers spoke up: "What? A whole month to tell the meaning of this text?" she exclaimed. "It is one of the nicest texts in the Bible." "Well, Mary," one of the ministers replied, "with your busy schedule, can you find time to pray continually?" "Yes," she answered, "the more I have to do, sir, the more time I find for my prayers." "Tell us, what do you mean?" the minister responded. "Well sir," said the young woman, "when I first open my eyes in the morning, I pray, 'Lord, open the eyes of my understanding.' While I am dressing, I pray that I may be clothed with the robe of Christ's righteousness. When I am washing, I ask to have my sins washed away. As I begin my work, I pray that I may receive strength for all the work of the day. While I kindle the fire, I pray that revival may be kindled in me. When preparing and eating breakfast, I ask to be fed with the Bread of Life and the pure milk of the Word. As I sweep the house, I pray that my heart may be swept clean of all its impurities. When I am busy with the children, I look up to God and pray that I may always have the trusting love of a little child; as I...."

"Enough!" interrupted the minister. "Go on Mary," he continued, "pray without ceasing. As for us, brothers, let us thank the Lord for this lesson."

By nature we pray sporadically because we trust ourselves so much. By grace, the closer we walk with the Lord the closer our prayer life will be with Him. To "pray without ceasing" reveals a walk with God that is constant. It points to the need to maintain regular times for daily prayer, without intermission. The more sporadic our walk with God is, the more sporadic our prayer life will be, and vice versa. Therefore, pray without ceasing—pray constantly.

23

PRAY DEPENDENTLY

Likewise the Spirit also helpeth our infirmities: for we know not what we should pray for as we ought: but the Spirit itself maketh intercession for us with groanings which cannot be uttered. And he that searcheth the hearts knoweth what is the mind of the Spirit, because he maketh intercession for the saints according to the will of God.
—ROMANS 8:26–27

True prayer is dependent prayer. We are to pray dependently, not independently. True prayer weans the petitioner from self-reliance. True prayer looks to the God of prayer—to the One who gives, hears, and answers prayer. Jesus Christ in heaven is the praying and interceding High Priest for His children; the Holy Spirit is the praying and interceding Spirit in their hearts. True prayer does not depend upon us.

A well-known story beautifully illustrates this truth. The captain of a ship was letting his son steer. When the captain noticed that they were going too far off course or too close to the rocks, or too near the sandbanks, he placed his hands over the hands of his son and the ship was turned. The boy was "steering," but his father actually guided the ship. It would have been foolish of this boy to worry or despair when seeing an island or narrow channel approaching. We would say to him, "Don't be alarmed, your father will guide you. He will not leave you alone to steer the ship." The son's anxiety developed when he mistakenly thought that he was steering the ship—as if everything depended upon him.

We, too, can so readily be filled with anxiety regarding our prayer life by thinking that we are at the helm, praying independently. When we see the approaching sandbanks of self-love, the rocks of lustful desires, the swift currents of spiritual pride, the islands of wandering thoughts, and the storms of our rebellious hearts, then we can become fearful and despondent. Though we must watch and pray against all of these approaching obstacles, when we fail we must not think our future is hopeless, or that we will never be able to steer around these dangers. Dear child of God, underneath these fears lies the unbelieving thought that if we do not steer properly, our heavenly Father will allow us to shipwreck and be cast away. We can struggle and strive so anxiously, foolishly, and independently, trying to guide our ship through life.

We are often like the apostles in the ship during the storm on the Sea of Galilee. They rowed hard and did everything to bring the ship to land, but could not. They were so foolish! They feared and despaired and exhausted themselves, and they did all this while Jesus was sleeping on board. Finally, at their wits' end, knowing that they could not safely bring the boat to shore by their own strength and skill, they cried out to Jesus, pleading for His help. Were all their fears and worries justified? With one word of Jesus' power, the storm was over and there was a great calm.

When the boy at the helm realizes his need and cries out for his father's help, will his father not respond? Of course.

His father saw the need and was responding before his son even cried out. Did the father not place his strong, experienced hands over his son's weak and inexperienced ones? Do you think that God the Father, by means of His Spirit, will be less loving, less ready to help the needy, less able to steer the ship than this human father? Sinful unbelief is so foolish! Belief and trust in God, not in self, hold the comfort, strength, and confidence of the Christian faith, including our prayer life. Prayer lies not in *our* hands; it does not depend on *our* skills. Prayer rests in placing our hand in our Father's hand, in relying upon the Holy Spirit's strength and skill. We are not called to pray independently, by our merits. If we were expected to do so, there would be reason for anxiety and despair. But the call to prayer, by God's grace, is to pray in dependency on the Holy Spirit.

24

UNFULFILLED PRAYER

I pray thee, let me go over, and see the good land that is beyond Jordan,…and the LORD said unto me, Let it suffice thee; speak no more unto me of this matter. Get thee up into the top of Pisgah, and lift up thine eyes westward, and northward, and southward, and eastward, and behold it with thine eyes: for thou shalt not go over this Jordan.

—DEUTERONOMY 3:25a, 26b, 27

For this thing I besought the Lord thrice, that it might depart from me. And he said unto me, My grace is sufficient for thee: for my strength is made perfect in weakness. Most gladly therefore will I rather glory in my infirmities, that the power of Christ may rest upon me.

—2 CORINTHIANS 12:8–9

Moses' prayer was legitimate. After forty years of leading the children of Israel through all the trials, difficulties, and setbacks they encountered in the wilderness, he now longed to rejoice in God's fulfillment; he desired to actually enter and see the land of Canaan. But the Lord denied his request because of his own act of anger and unbelief in smiting the rock twice. Though God forgave Moses, He said to him, "Let it suffice thee; speak no more unto me of this matter."

Paul's request was also legitimate. He experienced a constant thorn in the flesh, a handicap or impediment, and he asked God to remove it. Perhaps Paul thought he could serve the Lord more effectively if it was gone. But God's answer was, "My grace is sufficient for thee: for my strength is made perfect in weakness." In Paul's case, we read of no sin connected to God's lack of response.

These are biblical examples that legitimate prayers, proper requests, and fitting petitions can remain unfulfilled. It is possible that our prayers for wayward sons or daughters, for more effective gifts to serve, or for the healing of a loved one remain unfulfilled. Legitimate prayers may remain unfulfilled prayers. Such experiences can hang as a cloud over our spiritual lives. Everything begins to look darker and feel colder. We can become depressed, coming to wrong conclusions like, "All my prayers are fruitless," or "I must not be a child of God because my prayer is not answered." Both of these conclusions are mistaken. Remember that despite these examples of unfulfilled prayers, Moses and Paul were true children of God and many of their prayers were answered.

If our prayers do not obtain the benefits we desire, this does not necessarily mean that they are fruitless. Unfulfilled prayer can serve as a means to produce far deeper and more valuable benefits than those we originally requested. Unfulfilled prayer can teach us patience and contentment, surrendering and bowing before God. Moses did not rebelliously ascend Mount Nebo to look despairingly at the land and resentfully to die there. No, God was glorified more by Moses' response to his unfulfilled prayer than if it had been answered in the way he desired. Unfulfilled prayer can serve to exercise the soul and produce greater reliance upon God. Paul confessed, "When I am weak (in self), then am I strong (in the Lord)" (2 Cor. 12:10b). Whatever his thorn was, it kept him humble and dependent upon the Lord. Do you see how God provided richer experiences to Paul by not granting his request? The Lord can use unfulfilled prayer to work deeper fulfillment, rest, and trust in God. "My grace is sufficient for thee." A craftsman will be more glorified when he produces beautiful art with imperfect tools. Unfulfilled prayer can serve to teach us humility and dependency, to trust more in God and less in self. Unfulfilled prayer can loosen our attachment to man and temporal things.

Do you understand how unfulfilled prayer can produce rich, fulfilling purposes? And how fruitless prayer can serve a fruitful purpose? The difficulty lies with our vision. We often have our eyes on more shallow, temporary results and fruits. God's vision is deeper; He aims for eternal results and fruits. Moses' eye and prayer were focused upon earthly Canaan, which God denied; from Mt. Nebo, however, God took him into the heavenly Canaan. Paul desired that his temporary thorn be removed, but God gave him grace to bear it, and in the end Paul entered God's rest where all thorns are removed.

When considering unfulfilled prayers, let us remember that God's "no's" are often deeper "yes's." We may view unfulfilled prayer as receiving no answer from God, but He may be providing deeper answers. The Lord can fulfill much through unfulfilled payer, to His glory and to our amazement.

25

LUST-DRIVEN PRAYER

Ye ask, and receive not, because ye ask amiss, that ye may consume it upon your lusts.

—JAMES 4:3

"Ye ask" means "you pray." "Ye ask amiss," means "you pray wrongly or improperly." Why? Because you ask self-centeredly. You ask to fulfill your own desires and pleasures. Lustful prayer is improper prayer. In such prayer, we seek to gratify our desires to avoid suffering, to enhance our prestige, to further our own interests. Or, a child asks his parent if he may do a certain selfish thing. When the parent answers "No," the child may become angry and rebelliously grumble and sulk because he did not get his own lustful desire. Was this child really asking? Outwardly, he did ask his parent, but inwardly he told his parent what his self-centered plan should be. And because things did not go the way the child wanted and planned, he became very upset. So it is with improper prayer.

Let us honestly examine our prayer life. How many times do we ask like a spoiled child? We ask, but in reality we tell God what to do. When a heart is full of self-centeredness, it demands what it wants. In contrast, a heart full of love to God and others desires to sacrifice self and serve others. The lustful seeker asks that all trials and hardships may be avoided; the service-seeker asks for grace to serve and glorify the Lord in all circumstances that God places in his path. The self-seeker demands cure from illness; the God-seeker asks ultimately for patience and faithfulness in sickness or health so as to glorify God.

The critical difference between lustful and loving prayer lies in who is reigning as king in a person's heart. Only one can be on the throne. It is either *my* will or *Thy* will be done. When God is enthroned, self is dethroned. But the opposite is also true—when self is enthroned, God is dethroned. Have you ever realized what a rebellious, ugly, and perverted thing sin is? When we pray lustfully, we tell God what is right. A finite, weak, and sinful creature dares to tell the infinite, almighty, and holy Creator what to do or not do! Lustful prayer also reveals the sinful audacity to expect that He will do as we tell Him to do. Lustful prayer is sinful prayer; it is most improper. What would you think if a primary student told his teacher what to do, describing when, where, and how he wanted it done? What would you think if this child actually expected his teacher to do as he said? Do you see how disrespectful and rebellious such prayers sound in the Almighty's ears?

"Ye ask, and receive not, because ye ask amiss, that ye may consume it upon your lusts." Observe the rich paradox of spiritual truth here: we win when we surrender. "But seek ye first the kingdom of God, and his righteousness; and all these things shall be added unto you" (Matt. 6:33). We become the greatest in the kingdom when we are the least. We retain most when we give away most. Psalm 37:3–5 says, "Trust in the LORD, and do good; so shalt thou dwell in the land, and verily thou shalt be fed. Delight thyself also in the LORD; and he shall give thee the desires of thine heart. Commit thy way unto the LORD; trust also in him; and he shall bring it to pass."

In what spirit did you pray this morning? Did you pray, "God help me to be successful, honor me, make everything I do go well; Lord do 'this' for me and do not allow 'that' to happen"? Or did you pray, "God use me, help me to serve, and wherever Thou art leading me, oh Lord, help me to serve and glorify Thee"?

Improper prayer utilizes only the first part of Jesus' prayer in the Garden of Gethsemane, "if it be possible let this cup pass from me," but proper prayer includes and ultimately asks for the second part as well, "nevertheless not as I will, but as thou wilt" (Matt. 26:39b). The Lord Jesus never asks His children to endure more suffering, sorrow, or persecution than He did. Here He sets the example — to deny self and to glorify His Father.

Have you learned to pray *against* your old nature and *for* God? Spiritual warfare is real in true prayer. The new nature struggles to pray against and to subdue the old nature. Proper prayer strives to place both God and self in their rightful places — God on the throne and self as His servant. Improper prayer asks amiss; it prays lustfully. It places self on the throne and views God as a servant. Are you experientially acquainted with this spiritual battle to pray properly rather than improperly, to ask lovingly rather than lustfully?

26

PRAY OPENLY
AND UNWORTHILY

And the son said unto him, Father, I have sinned against heaven, and in thy sight, and am no more worthy to be called thy son.

—LUKE 15:21

This verse illustrates one of the most difficult lessons of prayer—to pray openly and penitently as an unworthy supplicant. This element determines whether prayer builds or relieves stress; whether you remain restless or receive peaceful rest. Picture two friends spending time together. Why is their time together restful and calming? Because they talk openly; they honestly confess their failures, discuss their faults, and pour out their frustrations. They do not have to prove themselves. They can safely rest in each other's friendship. They trust each other. In contrast, however, picture spending an evening with a person who is judging you—one to whom you must prove yourself, one to whose standards you must measure up. Would your time with this person be calming and restful, or would it be strenuous and stressful?

Private prayer is personal time with God. Do your prayer times build or relieve stress? Are they agitating or peaceful? Do they produce tension or rest? When prayer builds stress, it is because we do not trust the Lord and His free grace. We feel that we must prove ourselves to Him. Like Adam and Eve, we strain to sew "fig leaves" together to cover our failures. We do not pray openly and penitently. We also do not pray as someone who is unworthy. We struggle to prove our worth. We strain to produce true sincerity, proper feelings, fitting expressions, warm tears, and heartfelt repentances. The more we focus on self and our feelings, the more stress increases. The more self increases in importance, the more God decreases. The more "I" than "He" there is in our prayer, the more soul exertion there will be to make a positive impression upon the Lord.

Think about this. This is what we do when we speak with a stranger, someone we do not know or trust. But when we converse with a friend, we do not need to impress this friend, do we? We speak openly and trustingly. Do you pray openly with God? Do you freely confess your sins and unworthiness to the Lord? Do you unburden all your problems to Him? In prayer, do you bare your soul in His presence, or are you still hiding behind self-produced "fig-leaf-garments"?

Concealment produces anxiety, but open confession fosters rest. What a rest can be found near the heart of God! In prayer, we experience true rest in God when we confess (not hide) our failures, and relate (not conceal) our problems, and open (not close) our hearts in His presence. At such times we will experience that the Lord is a friend above all friends. His heart reveals an ocean of gracious love that knows no bounds. What rest the prodigal son found when he confessed all to his father! What peace he experienced when resting in his father's gracious love! And when did

Joseph's brothers experience the depth of love in Joseph's gracious heart? Was it when they strove to convince him that they were true and honest men? Or was it when they openly confessed their sins and unworthiness before him? In our prayer life, we also can miss the revelation of the Greater Joseph and His forgiving grace due to our attempts at concealing rather than confessing sin.

Do you trust the Lord? Do you pray openly and penitently as one who is unworthy? The more you pray this way, the more you will experience the peace and joy of prayer and the closer you will be drawn to the heart of God in His Son the Lord Jesus Christ, to His heart of free and sovereign grace. Seek grace to pray openly and unworthily.

27

PRAY AGAINST BESETTING SINS

And lead us not into temptation, but deliver us from evil.
—MATTHEW 6:13

Are you praying against your sins? Do you fear sin? Are you on guard against temptation, or do you flirt with sin? Each of us has a besetting sin or sins. These are sins that have a deep hold on and appeal to our hearts—sins that readily attract us or that we naturally fall into. These sins tempt us quickly, strongly, and frequently. One person's besetting sin might be coveting, e.g. another's car or money. For another, it may be pride in work accomplishments, or vanity about one's appearance. Besetting sins may come through accomplishments or abilities. They may be entertainment-focused, e.g., professional sports; they may include violent or sexual sins. In short, besetting sins reflect the lust of the flesh, the lust of the eye, or the pride of life.

The serious question facing each of us is: Do you and I pray against or skirt around our besetting sins in prayer? Do we strive to avoid or entertain this sin in practice? These two generally work together. For example, a person's besetting sin may be alcoholic drink. The more this person prays against this sin, the more he must strive to avoid the company and places where he is most likely to be tempted. If your beset-ting sin is coveting riches, the more you seriously pray against this sin, the more you must strive to be content with what you have as your portion from God and seek to avoid the company and places that promote anything that kindles these desires. If your besetting sin is sexually lustful thoughts, the more you pray against this sin, the more you must seek to avoid the company, places, and media that will foster this. These two must go together—your prayer and your walk.

Do you know what it means to pray "against yourself," to pray against the desires of your old nature? Do you feed or strive to starve your besetting sins? Do you know something of the struggle in prayer and life to overcome besetting sins? Some professed Christians speak confidently and victori-ously about conquering all sin but this is only self-conceit. If a soldier brags that he is always victorious, it indicates that he has not fought many battles. Sometimes the most profitable lessons can be learned from the most humiliating defeats. We must learn not to trust in our own strength and resolutions in this war against besetting sins. We need Jesus Christ. We need to pray against our old nature. The new nature must cry out for help against the old.

Paul describes this intense, personal warfare in Romans 7:21–24: "I find then a law, that, when I would do good, evil is present with me. For I delight in the law of God after the inward man: but I see another law in my members, warring against the law of my mind, and bringing me into captiv-ity to the law of sin which is in my members. O wretched man that I am! Who shall deliver me from the body of this death?" Everyone who prays and fights against sinful self will lose battles, but, by the grace of God, he will win the war. All such soldiers, struggling in prayer and life, will be victorious in their glorious Captain, their Lord and Savior Jesus Christ. This is why Paul could conclude, "I thank God through Jesus Christ our Lord" (Rom. 7:25a). In Christ he was sure to obtain victory in the end. So, fight on, pray on—pray against besetting sins.

28

PRAY FOR CONTENTMENT

Fear not, little flock; for it is your Father's good pleasure to give you the kingdom.
— LUKE 12:32

Be careful for nothing; but in every thing by prayer and supplication with thanksgiving let your requests be made known unto God. And the peace of God, which passeth all understanding, shall keep your hearts and minds through Christ Jesus.
— PHILIPPIANS 4:6–7

Biblical contentment means far more than being satisfied with our possessions, attainments, or relationships. Biblical contentment is not human; it is divine, for its source is faith in the promises of God. Obtaining biblical contentment is not easy and there are no shortcuts to it. But like the best of all divine blessings, we receive it, by the Spirit's grace, through steady and unwavering prayer (James 1:6). Contentment through prayer has many spiritual benefits; perhaps the most rewarding is the experience of peace, a peace that passes all natural understanding.

The first encouragement for finding contentment through prayer is the promise of the kingdom. In Luke 12, the Lord Jesus took great delight in dissuading the fears of

His people by encouraging them with the Father's willingness to give them the kingdom. Food and clothing are insignificant compared to "a treasure in the heavens that faileth not" (Luke 12:22). Worry and anxiety are not the way to obtain this kingdom; we can find it only through prayerful contentment and dependence on the Lord.

Another encouragement for believers to seek contentment through prayer is the spiritual peace and comfort that it gives in this life. The tenth commandment says, "Thou shalt not covet" anything belonging to your neighbor (Ex. 20:17). Covetousness creates strife and makes sinful demands of God (Ps. 78:18, 19; cf. Gal. 5:21; Rom. 14:17). But "godliness with contentment is great gain" (1 Tim. 6:6). Divine contentment takes our eyes off of worldly things, lifting them to the source of true happiness and fulfillment. That does not mean that all of our personal needs will be met, nor will it sweep us to heaven in human luxury. The secret of contentment, Paul says, is that it carries a believer in grace through thick and thin, plenty and want, sickness and health. Biblical contentment exclaims, "I can do all things through Christ which strengtheneth me" (Phil. 4:13). We can only realize this kind of contentment by praying and waiting on the Lord for His grace.

There are many obstacles to divine contentment. The first is our negative relationship to God's Law. Knowledge of sin comes through the Holy Spirit convicting us by the Law and sin takes advantage of the commandment to disrupt our communion with God (Rom. 3:20; 7:7–9). The only hope for us sinners, then, is to cast ourselves at the foot of the cross and ask for forgiveness in justification. Then, through the process of sanctification, we come to the throne of grace to ask for a contented heart.

The second obstacle to divine contentment is our lack of patience. Scripture teaches that tribulation works patience (Rom. 5:3). Patience and contentment, which take considerable endurance and maturity to cultivate, are closely related. Because we are not of those who shrink back, but who persevere in faith like those who have gone before us, we have the assurance that Christ will bring His work to completion in us. Psalm 138:8 says, "The LORD will perfect that which concerneth me: thy mercy, O LORD, endureth for ever: forsake not the works of thine own hands" (cf. Heb. 6:12; 10:39; Phil. 1:6).

Biblical contentment does not come naturally to fallen human beings. Contentment is a special gift of grace that believers should strive for in their private communion with God. Contentment will increase our faith and our joy in believing. It will also affect others whom God places along our life's pathway. Seek the grace of the Holy Spirit to pray with contentment.

But the Comforter, which is the Holy Ghost, whom the Father will send in my name, he shall teach you all things, and bring all things to your remembrance, whatsoever I have said unto you.

— JOHN 14:26

Scripture is the best support for a vibrant prayer life. From the beginning of our walk with Christ to the very end, the Holy Spirit leads us in knowledge and truth through Scripture. It may be tempting to think that knowledge of Scripture is secondary to our prayer life and communion with God. Some people say that Scripture was written in a primitive age and does not speak to our technologically advanced culture. Others assume that reading Scripture is merely an academic exercise, not a prayerful journey. But Scripture strengthens the spirit of prayer. Psalm 119:108 says, "Accept, I beseech thee, the freewill offerings of my mouth, O LORD, and teach me thy judgments." No theory of interpretation is so subtle that in prayer, the Spirit cannot lead us in all truth. And there was never a time when God's people did not depend on the Spirit for saving faith.

God inspired all Scripture: how does Scripture teach us to pray? How do we pray Scripture's promises? What does it mean to pray with Scripture? These questions need to move us to a greater dependence on the Holy Spirit and a lifelong pattern of praying Scripture promises and Scripture truth.

When the disciples asked the Lord Jesus how they should pray, He taught them a prayer that is the pattern of reverence and dependence (Matt. 6:9–13). The conclusion of the Lord's Prayer, "for thine is the kingdom," reminds us that we do not ask for material success. Instead, part of prayer is dependence on the Lord for the most basic things in life. The Lord's Prayer reminds us that God's forgiveness of sin and our forgiveness of others are as necessary to the Christian's daily life as food and clothing (Matt. 6:14; cf. 1 John 1:7). We learn to pray with Scripture rightly when we rest in God's sovereign pleasure to provide our needs, "for thine is the kingdom."

Paul's epistles offer more examples for praying with Scripture. The apostle consistently prayed for the church to grow in wisdom, the knowledge of Christ, and the hope of His great power (Eph. 1:15–19; Phil. 1: 3–6; Col. 1:9–10; 1 Thess. 1:2–5). Paul was confident that opposition from false teachers with impure motives would come to nothing; they could not harm God's people. Paul's confidence was the result of steadfast prayer for the Lord to lead His people in all wisdom and understanding.

The book of Psalms is also "the book of prayers." The Psalms are largely prayers in the form of songs. Singing, reading, and memorizing the Psalms can greatly enrich our prayer life.

Where else is wisdom more plain and pure than in Scripture? Scripture promises that any believer, especially one who lacks understanding, may ask God for wisdom, and "it shall be given him" (James 1:5). So, along with Paul, we learn to pray in the light of Scripture.

With many exhortations to pray, it is still possible for us to become discouraged with our prayer lives. Maybe you feel a deficiency in your desire to pray. Maybe you are affected by a sense of futility when you see the prosperity of the ungodly. From cover to cover, Scripture addresses these problems and offers the only solutions. Yes, sin carries natural consequences that teach the painful lesson, "you reap what you sow." But nature alone does nothing to encourage prayer; it cannot reveal the Spirit of prayer to our understanding the same way that Scripture does.

Consider a few examples from the Old Testament. Have you unjustly experienced the loss of property, work, or wealth? Psalm 37:7 tells you to rest confidently in the Lord and wait patiently for His deliverance. But Scripture also says, and warns you, that prayer is not only reserved for times of calamity. Job was keenly aware that God does not heed the ungodly man's prayer for deliverance because the ungodly neglect prayer altogether (Job 27:10).

Centuries later, the psalmist Asaph arrived at the same conclusion (Ps. 73:27). In considering the prosperity and ease of the wicked, the psalmist almost turned away from Scripture and prayer. But when he approached God in His sanctuary, Asaph freshly experienced God's mercy. He then uttered one of the most loving expressions to God in all of the Old Testament: "Whom have I in heaven but *thee*? and there is none upon earth that I desire beside thee" (Ps. 73:25). If reading Scripture was merely an academic exercise, the psalmist's words would simply be a moment of great poetry. But because it is God's inspired truth, it articulates one of the greatest realizations that comes in a believer's prayer life: that God is all in all. Paul echoed this great truth by saying that nothing can separate us from the love of God (Rom. 8:26, 31). No doubt the disciples also felt the power of this truth when Christ first taught them the Lord's Prayer.

Do you need instruction in how to pray? Encouragement to keep on praying? Guidance in how to pray, what to pray for? The words to express your desires? Look to Scripture, and learn to pray. Seek the Spirit's wisdom to pray with Scripture.

30

PRAY THOUGHTFULLY

I…will pray with the understanding.…
— 1 CORINTHIANS 14:15

*In the day when I cried thou answeredst me, and
strengthenedst me with strength in my soul.*
— PSALM 138:3

My people are destroyed for lack of knowledge.
— HOSEA 4:6

People have caricatured prayer as a shot in the dark, a last resort, or a superstitious ritual. Those views are demeaning to God, who has revealed Himself as the God who hears and answers prayer. God is not mocked; He closes His ears to the cry of the wicked, but sustains those who delight in His name (Ps. 34:15–16). Thoughtful prayer, like wisdom, begins with reverence and humility and ends with peace and pleasantness in the knowledge of God (cf. Job 28:28; Prov. 1:7; 3:17). Nothing can compare to the value of wisdom, and nothing quite cultivates, attains, or actively receives the knowledge of God more than thoughtful prayer (cf. Prov. 2:5, 6; James 1:5).

What does it mean to pray thoughtfully "with the understanding"? Prayer takes every part of our being to perform. Mind, will, spirit, and body posture all turn to God in a real and intimate way. Thoughtful prayer seeks to improve its understanding in sanctification, "being fruitful in every good work, and increasing in the knowledge of God" (Col. 1:10). Prayer turns the knowledge of God into action through obedience to God. Thoughtful, understanding prayer brings us into the presence of God in the hope of receiving blessing and communion.

How do we receive the knowledge of God in prayer? Thoughtful prayer acquires many benefits that education, unaccompanied by the Spirit, cannot obtain. Thoughtful prayer engages the Mediator, Christ Jesus, to receive strength, encouragement, and assurance of faith in the light of God's promises. Thoughtful prayer does not close its eyes in mere formality. Instead, it opens the soul's eyes to a panoramic view of God's benefits and promises recorded in Scripture. It offers us a view of Christ's exalted priesthood and an ever increasing sense of the Holy Spirit who enlarges our understanding and experience of the truth of God's will (cf. Ps. 103:2–5; Rom. 8:27, 28; Heb. 11:1).

Understanding thoughtless prayer clarifies what thoughtful prayer is. The Old Testament often characterizes unbelievers as those who do not pray, or if they do, their prayer is a last resort offered during a self-created calamity or carelessness. King Ahaz refused to ask God for a sign of deliverance and God allowed the Assyrians to bitterly betray and oppress him (Isa. 7:11, 12; 2 Chron. 28:21, 22). The books of Judges and Hosea correctly attribute the calamity that befell ancient Israel to her neglect and abandonment of the knowledge of God (Judges 2:10, 11). Again and again, the children of Israel cried out to God when they could no longer endure suffering at the hands of their oppressors. These examples should not discourage us from praying, for, the psalmist tells us, God listened to those prayers and responded to them: "Nevertheless, he regarded their affliction, when he heard their cry: and he remembered for them his covenant, and repented according to the multitude of his mercies" (Ps. 106:44, 45).

Prayer is not an emergency 911 call. It should never be thought of as a hotline to God. Thoughtful prayer is mutual communion that reciprocates the covenant bond between Christ, the head of the church, and His people. Believers must be ever conscious of their need for deliverance from sin and death (Rom. 7:18, 24). They must wait prayerfully for the Lord to accomplish His will (Rom. 8:24).

God knows your needs before you speak them (Ps. 139:4). He knows all about you, for His knowledge is omniscient. David prayed in the light of God's knowledge (Ps. 139) and received the remarkable assurance that God was guarding his steps in every circumstance (v. 12). That should encourage us to pray thoughtfully. Thoughtful prayer moves us from weakness to strength and from strength to glory. It binds us to God and comforts us in distress. Pray not as a last resort, but in the increasing knowledge of God and His will. Pray thoughtfully "with the understanding" (1 Cor. 14:15).

31

CONCLUSION:
TO THOSE WHO CANNOT PRAY

Come unto me, all ye that labour and are heavy laden, and I will give you rest.

— MATTHEW 11:28

When closing these meditations on prayer, you may end up feeling very discouraged because you must honestly confess, "I cannot pray as I should, so I cannot pray at all." Every one of the previous meditations condemns you. Turn to Jesus' words in Matthew 11:28: "Come unto me, all ye that labour and are heavy laden, and I will give you rest."

If you labor to produce believing, submissive, intercessory, thankful, and fervent prayers and only become more heavy laden, discouraged, downcast, and depressed, listen to these words of the Savior. If you feel your burden increase weekly, recognizing that your prayers are far from what they should be; if you are heavy laden because you know you do not labor enough; if you are discouraged because you cannot stir up or encourage your heart to pray as you should, then hear these words of Christ. If you find that you are filled with self instead of God when you try to pray, that your mind wanders from God instead of focusing on Him, and that temporal concerns crowd out eternal needs so many times—listen, listen to the Word of God! Jesus invites, yes, lovingly commands all such laboring and heavy laden ones. He tenderly instructs them: "Come unto me."

Imagine for a moment, a hard-working businessman who struggles in business, but after all his labors day and night, he cannot meet the interest payment due on his debt. Each year, at the end of all his strenuous work, his debt has increased rather than decreased. This man has been struggling for years to be successful and he refuses to acknowledge defeat. Is this a picture of your endeavors spiritually? Are you such a spiritual laborer? At the close of each year do you only discover more debt, despite all your strenuous work to produce the fruits of true prayer? Are you collapsing under the realization that in all your praying there is no true prayer? Jesus speaks to people who labor under an ever-increasing load. Christ says, as it were, "Declare spiritual bankruptcy. You will never be able to clear your own account. Plead for mercy with Me. I have an infinite account of grace. I will fully pay and free you from all your debts."

"Come unto me." Do not turn to yourself for rest, but "Come unto me…and I will give you rest." Jesus' words here are not "maybe," but "I will." It is as if He asks: "Why, heavy-laden one, do you still cling to self? Why do you keep thinking and hoping that somehow you will yet be able to clear your own debt? Why do you continue to trust yourself more than Me? *I* will give you rest—not *you*. Rest in My payment—not in yours. Salvation will never be found in your prayers. It is only found in mine, in My high priestly prayer. My prayers perfectly fulfill all the meditations you read and many more. If you are a burdened sinner "that thirsteth, come ye to the waters, and he that hath no money; come ye, buy, and eat; yea, come, buy wine and milk without money and without price. Wherefore do ye spend money for that which is not bread? And your labour for that which satisfieth not? hearken diligently unto me, and eat ye that which is good, and let your soul delight itself in fatness (Isa. 55:1–2).

Heavy-laden soul, do not let Satan deceive you. Do not try to change God's covenant of grace into one of works. Do not pollute His grace with your works. Do not say, "I have not labored enough yet; I am not yet heavy laden enough." Every child of God under conviction of the Spirit will confess that he does not labor enough and is not heavy laden enough. He will readily confess that in himself there is nothing to be found but shortcomings and sins. Do not lean on your own calculations. Do not trust in your own feelings. Do not judge by your own measurements. Trust solely upon the gracious words of the Savior who cannot lie: "Come unto me, all ye that labour and are heavy laden, and I will give you rest."

Declare your bankruptcy. Trust His fullness. Salvation lies in free and sovereign grace. His labors need to swallow up yours; His prayers need to absorb yours. Therefore, pray—especially when you feel like you cannot pray. Bankruptcy is the time for mercy. It is the wonderful work of the Holy Spirit to bring together an empty sinner and a full Christ. You cannot find salvation in what you do for the Lord, but salvation is secure in what He has done for you. You will never find rest in your prayers to Him. His prayers for you are the only ones that can save your soul and keep you in the circle of His grace for this life and for a better life to come in glory. *Soli Deo gloria!*

31 MARKS OF TRUE PRAYER

1. True prayer brings heaven down into the soul and lifts the soul up to heaven.

2. True prayer is the prime exercise of faith where all saving graces converge to climax in both the highest expression of gratitude (to God) and the deepest expression of humility (with regard to ourselves), as well as the broadest expression of love (for others).

3. True prayer is real life. It is spiritual air for spiritual lungs. Thomas Watson described it as "the soul's breathing itself into the bosom of its heavenly Father." Where prayerless praying overtakes prayerful praying, the true believer degenerates into listlessness.

4. True prayer is the sinner's response to God's voice. The prayer of the brokenhearted is a gift to God in reply to God's gift of prayerful brokenheartedness. True prayer is returning to God through the weaknesses and stains of human brokenness and unworthiness what God has decreed from all eternity, made room for in time, and brought to fruition in the moment of actual soul-wrestling.

5. True prayer is a holy art taught by a groaning, wrestling Spirit who often uses the impossibilities and apparent "artlessness"

of the believer's entangled and sin-stained life to pencil upon him the image of his worthy Master.

6. True prayer is the fruit of God Triune—the Father as Giver and Decreer, the Son as Meritor and Perfector, the Spirit as Wrestler and Indweller.

7. True prayer has an unexplainable way of augmenting both the worthiness of Christ and the unworthiness of the sinner; hence, it is both the chief part of humility and of thankfulness (cf. Heidelberg Catechism, Q. 116).

8. True prayer is the believer's greatest weapon in the armory of God. Puritan Thomas Lye confessed: "I had rather stand against the canons of the wicked than against the prayers of the righteous."

9. True prayer does not preach to God. It does not lead by the hand, but reaches for His guiding hand.

10. True prayer has more to do with God than man. It is wrapped up in holy concern for the glory and kingdom of God. It does not focus upon itself or the petitioner. It does not turn inward for morbid introspection, but turns inward to bring all the sinner's deadness and depravity outward and upward to the Almighty God of grace.

11. True prayer longs for revival. Its expectation is only in the Lord. When Adoniram Judson had labored for eight years without one apparent convert, his Mission Board sincerely asked him if he had any expectation left. An affirmative answer prompted the question: "But how great is your expectation?" Judson responded: "As great as the promises of God."

12. True prayer lets God be God. It empties its hands and heart before the open throne of God. It hides nothing. True prayer is not explanation but petition. It doesn't tell the Lord how to

convert a sinner, but asks Him to do it, trusting He knows better than any petitioner.

13. True prayer spreads out everything before the Lord as if He knows nothing about the sinner's condition, yet knowing that the Lord knows all.

14. True prayer conjoins holy reverence and holy familiarity with holy boldness.

15. True prayer is not self-congratulatory, but self-condemnatory and Christ-congratulatory.

16. True prayer recognizes that it changes neither God nor "things," while simultaneously realizing that God often is pleased to reach His purposes through the means of prayer.

17. True prayer is fellowshipping with God. It is a foretaste of heaven's eternal conversation.

18. True prayer is not a flurry of words in an ever-spiralling height of voice, but it is a matter of the heart in an ever-spiralling depth of meditation and pause before God.

19. True prayer ever feels that it is not sufficiently deep, thorough, and unbosoming.

20. True prayer, when neglected, is like an untapped power line, a disconnected computer, a system broken down. Valuable information neither descends or ascends.

21. True prayer dresses itself in words, but its body is wordless. It is heart-work. Hence, Bunyan rightly advises: "When thou prayest rather let thy heart be without words than thy words without a heart."

22. True prayer measures no need too great or too small. It neither assumes human probability nor flinches in the face of human impossibility.

23. True prayer senses the presence of divine majesty and human dust-and-ashes cohabiting. This cohabitation causes the sinner to take his shoes from off his feet, for the place of true prayer is holy ground.

24. True prayer pleases God. It shows Him the divine handwriting of Scripture and the divine signature of His covenant promises. As William Gurnall states: "Prayer is nothing but the promise reversed, or God's Word formed into an argument, and retorted by faith upon God again." John Trapp adds: "Prayer is putting the promises into suit."

25. True prayer profoundly feels that its authenticity can only be validated by the praying High Priest, Christ Jesus, who salts imperfect petitionings with the salt of His meritorious sufferings before presenting the church's prayers without spot or wrinkle in His holy Father's sight. Thomas Adam wrote: "I put my prayers into Christ's hands; and what may I not expect from them, when I have such an Advocate? Oh, be sure not to ask a little from God!"

26. True prayer brings particular requests and waits for particular answers. And they shall be answered—perhaps not immediately, but God's delays are not His denials. Scripture does say of the Canaanitish woman's first pleading, "But he answered her not a word," but it does not say, "But he heard not a word." True prayer is never lost, even if it be forgotten. "God never denied that soul anything that went as far as heaven to ask it" (John Trapp).

27. True prayer "brings God into the heart and keeps sin out.... Prayer is knowing work, believing work, thanking work,

searching work, humbling work, and nothing worth if heart and hand do not join in it.… Want felt and help desired, with faith to obtain it, is prayer.… One prayer is worth a thousand fine thoughts…" (Thomas Adam).

28. True prayer is bathed in faith. Faithless prayer is fruitless prayer, no matter how sincere it may be. True prayer is the fruit of true faith and true faith is the fruit of true prayer. Faith and prayer are best of friends who build up each other for they have a common goal—the glory of the worthy, Triune God.

29. True prayer is often short, frequent, and repetitive, sometimes hardly getting beyond the simple words, "Lord, Lord… have mercy."

30. True prayer for others also reaps great benefits for the petitioner in a feeling sense of his own closeness with God. True prayer can't intercede explicitly for others without praying implicitly for one's self.

31. True prayer is a joy in itself even when the answer to come may appear to contradict the very petitions offered. As William Gurnall said, "'Tis a mercy to prayer, even when I don't receive the mercy prayed for." But if unanswered prayer is sweet, how much sweeter is answered prayer. Joseph Hall wrote, "Good prayers never come weeping home; I am sure I shall receive either what I ask or what I should ask."

Lord, teach us to pray.